A JOHN CATT PUBLICATION

EDUCATING DREW

THE REAL STORY OF HARROP FOLD SCHOOL

First Published 2017

by John Catt Educational Ltd,
12 Deben Mill Business Centre, Old Maltings Approach,
Melton, Woodbridge IP12 1BL

Tel: +44 (0) 1394 389850 Fax: +44 (0) 1394 386893
Email: enquiries@johncatt.com
Website: www.johncatt.com

ISBN: 978 1 911382 32 4

Set and designed by John Catt Educational Limited

"An honest and refreshing account of leading a school in challenging circumstances. Drew demonstrates his relentless determination and passion to improve the community of Little Hulton in an inspiring and entertaining tale. A must-read for anyone working in schools."

Dan Roberts, Headteacher at Devonport High School for Boys, Plymouth

"Once I started reading this book, I found it annoyingly hard to put down! It's not really a leadership book. Nor is it a book about how to do school improvement. Instead, it is a disarmingly honest and charming account of the joys and challenges of working in a difficult but intensely rewarding school community. Drew describes his own leadership approach as quirky. And it probably isn't everyone's cup of tea. But knowing he was a right pain at school himself and, for example, seeing him giggling at the (by now) legendary #VanGate incident alongside turning the school round, makes this a delightful read from cover to cover."

Andy Buck, Managing Director #honk; Founding Director, Leadership Matters

"Utterly gripping and very funny. An account of how it is possible to transform schools and communities through strength of will, humanity and absolute perseverance. A must-read for all in the sector."

Mary Myatt, author, school adviser

Contents

Introduction

In my early career I was a teacher and, in so many ways, it has stood me in good stead for my current career in international rugby. Whether leading a team of professional athletes, an international business or a school – there are a number of common skills and principles that are necessary to achieve success, however that is measured.

I have known Drew for a number of years and we have discussed the issues of leading through challenging change. Drew has a wealth of knowledge and a depth of understanding of a range of leadership concepts and he is adept at applying this across a range of situations and sectors.

The story of Harrop Fold and Drew's leadership of the school is inspirational and I would encourage people to read it, learn from it and maybe let it help them improve their own leadership in whatever context they work. The school still has its challenges, but I truly believe that Team Harrop will win in the end, against all odds!

Warren Gatland

Warren Gatland
Head Coach of the British and Irish Lions

Foreword

It is hard to believe that it was six years ago that I was hiding behind my sofa cushion watching the first episode of *Educating Essex*. The memories of the explosion of interest that happened after are so vivid; from the huge increase in the number of selfies I was requested to be in through to the visitors that were suddenly interested in coming to see us at Passmores.

In the years that have followed many people have asked me 'why'? Why did we say yes in the first place to having over 15,000 hours of our school life recorded? Normally this is followed by 'you were brave'. It is at this point that I wish I could read minds because I am convinced that if I could they would be saying 'brave? – more like mad/egotistical/trying to earn out of it' (delete as applicable).

I think the headteachers and governing bodies from the schools that have followed have been the brave ones. They have known what they are letting themselves in for. They have known that the national press will have a strong opinion of them and that the local press will get very excited indeed!

I have enjoyed being involved, from a distance, in the series that have followed ours through writing articles *etc* but also by being able to talk to my fellow heads to share our experience prior to them going through it. So when I got a direct message, through Twitter, from Drew Povey I was delighted to have a chat. After only a couple of conversations it was hard to have a strong opinion of what Drew was going to be like in his edited form and how Harrop Fold would 'feel' but I thought his passion and commitment would shine through. Being given the chance to read this book prior to the series going out confirmed that view and having seen just one episode as I write this I am so pleased that I was right.

The similarities between our two schools are quite remarkable. Passmores took on 300 students in one year from a school that was closed locally, for instance, in a similar way to which Harrop Fold was an amalgamation of two schools. In fact, I'd go as far as to say that this *Educating...* series has a really comfortable and welcoming feel that reminds me more of our series than any of the others so far.

So what are you going to learn from reading this book?

It only takes you to read the Prologue to know that the book pulls no punches and is brutally honest throughout; it is as plain speaking and straight forward as Drew and his team come across on television. Working in education, in any school, is challenging; working in education in schools in Harrop Fold's setting magnifies those challenges especially, as the book makes very clear, if you add in the lack of investment from successive governments to areas outside of London and the south east of England. However, do not for one second think that this book is one that is going to make you feel worse for reading it; that it is a book full of 'woe is me' rhetoric about how hard it is for them - the 'brothers' and the rest of the community. It is not. I nodded and smiled throughout reading it.

As Drew and the staff of Harrop Fold have shown us, through our TV screens, the interactions between staff and students remain such an opportunity to make a difference to the students. The adults and young people that you have probably already fallen in love with, however, are not characters in a TV drama. What you see going on in their lives is real as are the laughter and tears.

There is so much that I want to say having read this book but I don't want to be the 'spoiler'. The truth is that whether you have no interest in becoming a teacher but just loved the series or you are considering joining our profession this will book will resonate and educate. If you are an evangelist for the 'no excuses' approach that is gaining much coverage in the media, you will probably hate this book but should read it nevertheless to just give yourself a counter viewpoint to consider. Finally, if you are thinking about whether or not you wish to become a headteacher I am certain that you will finish this book having learned a great deal about Drew, Ross, Ben and the cast of thousands at Harrop Fold but should also be considering, even more seriously, the prospect of dedicating your career to reimagining what is possible to achieve with young people – ALL young people – and making it happen.

Vic Goddard
Head of Passmores Academy
September 2017

Prologue

Working as a headteacher in Little Hulton, a small area of Salford in the North-West of England, is amazing. At our school, Harrop Fold, the kids are superb, the staff are astounding, the community is supportive. Wherever I go I tell people that special things are happening in Little Hulton.

To an outsider, this sort of positive attitude can come as a surprise. If they have heard of it at all, they usually only know Little Hulton because of bad news headlines or the high levels of poverty in the area. Or they might remember that Harrop Fold was once labelled 'the worst school in the country'. That was back when eight in 10 children were leaving without five GCSE passes to their name and hundreds of pupils were being excluded each month.

Let's not sugarcoat it, those things are all true.

They do not give the true picture of Little Hulton, though. What those newspaper stories neglected to mention were the thousands of people who live there and do amazing things every day. From the kids who come through our gates, to the teachers working with them, the parents looking after them, the police making sure they are safe. Little Hulton is a small place, but it is mighty.

When the *Educating Greater Manchester* team came to our school, they saw this special thing we've built. The TV show, hopefully, will let you in to see some of it too. And, no doubt, you'll see my two brothers, Ross and Ben, who also work at the school with me now, and who did so back when kids were being frogmarched into police vans at lunchtime because fights were breaking out on a daily basis.

Harrop Fold is not like this anymore. Now, the proportion of pupils passing their GCSEs has tripled and we no longer exclude any young people. None. We have changed the school's fortunes without giving up on any kid. Something I defy almost any other school to say they achieved.

But don't be fooled into thinking this turnaround has been brought about solely by Ross, Ben and myself. Three brothers working together make for a neat phoenix-from-the-ashes story, especially as we are all very different and none of us started out thinking that we would become teachers. We did not turn the school around alone, however. For a start, Dr Anthony Edkins was the headteacher who hired all three of us and started the transformation. Then there's the cast of thousands – staff, parents, pupils, governors, local shopkeepers, grandparents, the police – who all played their part.

So Harrop Fold isn't the story of three brothers. It's the story of how three brothers, and *thousands* of others turned around a school.

It takes a village to raise a child. It took somewhere as special as Little Hulton to raise an entire school from the depths it found itself in.

Despite all the hard work to get to this point, however, the school is now facing an injustice that I, and my brothers, and our community, can no longer ignore. Harrop Fold has a debt of approximately £1.5 million which it must pay back. Originally, it was £3.1 million. Over the past seven years we managed to pay off well over a million by cutting staff to the bone, and pushing class sizes as high as 36 (in classrooms designed only to take 30). We've shaved pennies off postage, we've cut back on utilities. But if we keep cutting then it will be the children of Harrop Fold who suffer.

The debt is also stopping us from doing things which don't cost any money and would help the children. For example, we know that while behaviour is now sorted in the school, we need some help to improve the curriculum – and make sure the lessons we are offering can match the standards set in England's very best schools, which tend to be clustered outside the North-West, often in wealthier places, such as London.

How this came about, and why it can't be solved, is an intriguing story. I will explain in the pages of this book how decisions made before today's schoolkids were even born are having a devastating, long-term impact on their education. Frankly, it's a disgraceful situation and – as you will see – one that is entirely solvable. Other schools have been treated very differently to ours – especially those in the capital city, and those connected in some way to a person of influence. That is fundamentally unfair, and ought to be resolved.

But debt is not the main reason we said yes to the *Educating Greater Manchester* series. What we wanted, more than anything, was for people across the country to see how special our school, our kids, and our community really is. It's the people that make Little Hulton special. It's the people, in everything, that truly make the difference.

Chapter 1 –
Let's start at the start

'Don't wish it were easier, wish you were better' – Jim Rohn, entrepreneur

In September 2001, two planes hit the Twin Towers in New York. By coincidence, that same month, Harrop Fold School first opened its doors.

Created out of two schools, a mile apart, whose pupil rolls were falling, the merger caused uproar in the local area. One of the schools that would become Harrop was doing okay. Joseph Eastham School had around four in 10 pupils leaving school with five GCSE passes. In the context of today, where the national average is much higher, that sounds bad. In 2001 it was normal.

Little Hulton County High School was much worse. Around one in every 10 pupils left with five GCSEs. Think that through for a minute. Let it sink in. If you sat all the young people in assembly in rows of 10 – nine of each row were walking out the door with fewer than five C grades at GCSE, which is the minimum you need to get into college. Even on-the-job apprenticeships typically want to see five GCSE passes. Yet, at that time, nine out of 10 left with almost nothing.

So, the council decided to push the two schools together. It seemed a sensible solution, except the communities didn't particularly like each other. There was a long-term rivalry between the schools and some families, on either side, were mortal enemies. Their children were thrown together, without regard for such problems, or any plans to solve Little Hulton's issues.

Even worse, the council kept both school sites – which were around a mile apart. A decision was taken to teach key stage 3 pupils (children aged between 11 and 14) on one site, and then to put the GCSE year groups on the other. To make this split work, staff had to be shuttled back and forth, and pupils travelled each day on public buses from their home estates to the new school sites. Behaviour was so bad on those bus trips – swearing, fighting and so on – that in the end the bus company refused to even pick students up. The only way to resolve it was to get police officers and staff travelling with them. You know you have hit a deep low when the law have to be called in to keep children coming to school.

The merger divided the community. Parents complained bitterly. Many good teachers fled, leaving behind those who either couldn't get a job elsewhere or couldn't be bothered to do so. A few stand-out teachers dug their heels in and stayed, but classroom learning was going down the pan. Crowd control was about the best anyone could manage.

Even worse, bullying became prevalent. Corridors reeked of cigarette smoke. Local shops banned the children due to the level of thieving. The school sites ended up becoming the priority hub for the pool of four schools-based police officers in the local area.

By 2003 things were so bad that a third of pupils had stopped turning up regularly. The full-time attendance rate dropped to 71 per cent. On an average day, a teacher could expect around nine children out of a class of 30 to be absent. Think about that in terms of names. Imagine reading out the register and every third kid fails to say 'here'. It's utterly demoralising.

Eventually the complaints caught the eye of England's school inspectorate, Ofsted. Fifteen inspectors flooded into the school gates and watched the pupils and staff over several days. It did not go well. One afternoon the lead inspector narrowly escaped (via an open door) a scrum of boys charging down the corridor. At the end of the day, the inspectors announced the school was to be given the worst possible rating: special measures.

The report from that inspection is damning, and rightly so. 'The school provides a very poor standard of education,' it begins. 'Few students receive the education to which they are entitled.'

Behaviour was out of control. In the 12 weeks before the inspectors arrived, 137 pupils had been excluded for at least one day. Four had been turned away for good.

Some of the most vulnerable pupils were being treated the worst. Lower-attaining students were put onto a vocational gardening course that had no resources. Pupils had spent two years sowing vegetables. Those who arrived latest to the lesson had to collect litter for the whole day as no plots of land were available to them.

Respect was missing, the report continues – not just between the kids and the staff, but between the kids themselves. The young people had little ability to take responsibility for their behaviour.

The report carries on like this for 56 pages. I'm not always sympathetic to Ofsted's views as I think they can be out of touch, but I'm not going to be an apologist for what was going on at Harrop Fold. The pupils were being severely let down. Teachers and governors didn't believe they could do better. That was an injustice.

A few years after this low point, I learned that the Chair of Governors was told by a government official that Harrop Fold was considered 'the worst school in the country'.

That 2003 inspection was a wake-up call that started something special which has been burning brightly ever since. Turnaround took a long time and, to my mind, it's still going. Incremental improvements are what we are aiming for every day. We can always be better.

But by 2010, the school was finally rated 'good', and it was again in 2013. More importantly, far more importantly, we changed the culture. We stopped the ridiculous exclusions. We put a stop to the cigarettes. Police officers no longer need to ride with our students because they can trust them to behave.

In our school now, pupils care for each other. Still-feuding families put aside their differences and sit next to each other on parents' evening ready to hear how their child is getting on. Come and see our staff who give everything to our pupils; pupils who listen, and learn, and are respectful.

At Harrop Fold today, we've done exactly what New York architects had to do when the Twin Towers came down. We didn't just re-build, we re-imagined. Now if you come to our school you will see a community full of people who, day-in and day-out, are making the difference. Because it's always the people who make the difference.

So that's the story of how Harrop Fold School began.

But what's the story of how we brothers got involved? For that, we need to go further back in time.

'We determine our circumstances; our circumstances don't determine us'

I was born two years after my brother Ross in the October of 1977. Ross doesn't remember the day. He does remember when Ben was born, some years later, in 1985. He had been sent to stay with our Gran and had taken along his *Star Wars* toys to play with. When it was time to come visit his new little brother he wanted to bring his Luke Skywalker figure which Gran, being the sensible lady she was, made him boil first to eliminate any germs before giving it to me. That story nicely foreshadows how much Ross would act sensibly in those early years, while I was busy causing bother.

All three of us grew up in Stockton Heath, a quaint village on the outskirts of Warrington, in the North-West of England. The village was originally a Roman settlement, and it's a parish area now – with nice churches, including the one my family attended each weekend. It's also the place where George Formby, the famous WWII entertainer, was raised. If you've ever heard his northern accent, you'll have some idea of how Ross and Ben and I all sound!

Our dad was a disciplinarian. He was a teacher in a secondary school, and was known for wielding the cane ferociously. He was strict with us boys. Ross avoided most of it as our parents always said they only had to look at him and he would do the right thing. I was naughtier and received serious scoldings. These days, when I'm telling a pupil off at school, I can sometimes hear dad's words starting to come out of my own mouth. When he would shout up the stairs for us boys to come downstairs for dinner, and we'd respond with 'we're coming', he'd always say in a deadpan voice, 'yeah, so is Christmas'. It's a terrible dad-joke, yet I hear myself say it all the time to pupils who are dawdling.

Our mum was at home looking after us three boys for many years. It's a good job she was there, as I think we were a bit of a handful. Later, when we were all at secondary school or beyond, she also went into teaching of a sort. She became a teaching assistant, then a learning mentor, before finally working with children in alternative provision.

If you're thinking teaching was in our blood, though, you're dead wrong. Nothing was further from our minds when we were growing up. We wanted to be footballers and musicians, definitely. Teachers? Never.

Out of the three of us, I would have said that I was the one least likely to wind up in education. My primary school struggled with my challenging behaviour. Ross, on the other hand, was always brainy.

We both attended Stockton Heath Primary School and back then every kid in the county had to take an exam called the Cheshire Primary Tests, which were used to rank you against every other child of your age. Ross came out in the top 5% of the county. I did much, much worse.

Ben was always fairly good at school. Unfortunately for him, staff found it hard to forget my challenging behaviour so I was a tough act to follow for Ben, which wasn't really fair on him I guess. But, like Ross, he was very bright and picked things up quickly and so staff got to like his cheeky-chap persona. Ben's a very quick-witted guy but he can sometimes go too far!

Learning my academic ranking compared to other young people really affected my confidence. Why would anyone tell a kid they're so far behind when they're that young? As a consequence, instead of working hard at school, I focused on being entertaining.

Ross, meanwhile, was top of the class and never once misbehaved. The only thing he ever did that drove people daft was take things apart. Toys, machines, plugs, anything he could get his hands on. Not in a destructive way: he just wanted to understand how they work. Even now, if you're sitting in a meeting with Ross, he'll start taking his pen apart. He removes the springs, dismantles the clicker. It's annoying, but everyone saw it as a signal of him being smart. Ross was very much seen as the 'clever boy'. Meanwhile, I stammered and struggled with reading. I was definitely the 'naughty boy'.

It's a bit hard to admit that side of my childhood now. When you're the headteacher of a school you want to be a great behaviour role model. But the truth is that my behaviour as a kid was bad. Not malicious or aggressive. I never, ever swore. But I pushed boundaries and challenged rules all the time. Ross describes my years at primary school as 'a continuous assault on middle-aged ladies'. It's a bit of a dramatic way to put things as I never hit anyone, but I was constantly wriggling around, asking questions, not doing my work. When poor Ross would come by, to check up on me, I'd make silly noises and call him Billy Brown Trousers – really immature stuff. Almost every teacher refused to have me in their classroom for more than an hour as it was so exhausting trying to keep me still and stop me distracting others.

Mrs Firth was the only teacher who put a stop to that. She was brilliant. I couldn't spell many words in primary school but I could spell her name. F-I-R-T-H, the best word in the world. I adored her. In the end I spent most of my time in primary school with her. While the other teachers rotated me around, Mrs Firth would have me for any amount of time, and I always did what she said.

Why? Looking back, it's the little things that stand out in terms of what she did to get me onside. For example, my stammer made it difficult for me to answer the register. As a kid that's a horrible thing to face each day. I would be sat there, waiting for my name to be read out and start panicking. It's a pretty terrible feeling when you already don't have much confidence in your abilities and then you can't even communicate that you exist. There was Ross, winning at tests, and there's me, unable even to answer to my name. Mrs Firth found a work around that saved face.

When she got to my name she would find some other way to acknowledge me. She might say something like 'I see Drew is already here', or maybe miss my name out and nod at me, or ask me to do an errand when she got to me instead. Always, always she found a way. That meant everything to me. It meant Mrs Firth had noticed me as an individual, not as a stereotypical 'naughty boy' and she'd helped me sort my problem. Not by making a big deal out of things, but by helping me. I owed her for that. And I was never naughty with Mrs Firth.

My parents found my behaviour exasperating too. There's a famous story about me and a blancmange. A wobbly, pink, rabbit blancmange to be precise. It was the 1980s after all.

It was a Sunday and our parents had invited people around for dinner. This was normal for us. Mum and dad were very involved in the church, so people often arrived for food and a catch-up. I liked the company enormously as I have always liked talking to people and although I was a handful I was typically well-liked by our parents' friends.

On this particular day, however, mum had made a surprise. It was a blancmange in the shape of a large bunny rabbit. She put in on the table, still encased in its huge metal mould, before proudly whipping it off to reveal said pink bunny rabbit, wobbling away on the plate.

Mum needed to go to the kitchen to get bowls but there was a problem. She and I both knew that I would want to spoil her creation.

As I reached out my finger to give it a push, mum turned and wagged her finger directly at me. 'Do NOT touch it,' she said.

That was a bad move. Telling me not to do things, even as an adult, is like waving a red flag at a bull. No sooner had she turned her back than I leaned over and put my finger right through the centre of the rabbit. I got away with it, too, as Ross never told on me!

Now, as a senior school leader, I know how these small misdemeanours gradually wear you down. It's also not a good mindspace for a kid to get into. It's like those experiments with young children who lack the discipline to sit and look at a marshmallow without eating it; when they have been promised a second treat if they can wait, they tend to go on and do less well in the future. Likewise, if you're in a classroom and a kid keeps doing things they shouldn't – standing up, turning around, whatever – it is really disruptive to learning and suggests they haven't learned the discipline they need to succeed in the future. It's up to you as an adult to help them acquire that self-restraint. You just don't realise that when you're six and wobbling a bunny rabbit seems the funniest thing in the world.

Eventually my misbehaviour at school came to a head. The teachers didn't know how to deal with me anymore. My mum negotiated with the school to stop me being excluded. My behaviour had to change though, and so the dog I'd always wanted was just around the corner.

During my last year at primary school my parents gifted me a massive black Labrador, who I called Carrie. She was wriggly and gorgeous and my responsibility. 'This is your dog,' they told me. 'You are going to be responsible for it, you are going to feed it, and you are going to walk it each day.'

As a side note, I tell people the dog was named Carrie after the same-named song by Europe, who did the song 'The Final Countdown'. I'd say you should put this book down and go listen to it now for context, but I don't want to be responsible for ruining your day. If you ever hear this story from Ross, he will tell you the dog was named after 'Carrie doesn't live here anymore' by Cliff Richard, but that's just him trying to embarrass me.

The dog was an absolutely genius plan. I loved the routine and discipline. I had always loved sport, because I love moving about, so walking her was no problem. Plus this was something that I could be good at. Reading and writing were difficult, but I could look after a dog. It made me feel proud to be responsible for something other than myself.

Over the years, it's a trick that I've used often with kids. Not so much getting them a dog, although I have recommended pets on occasion, but, more broadly, getting young people to have responsibility for something beyond themselves. We are inherently quite selfish beings and we tend to think about ourselves first (at least until we become parents). When I put my finger through that bunny, I was purely thinking about what I wanted to do and not about the impact on my mum who had spent time making the thing. There's loads of ways to get students thinking beyond their own life, whether it's working with a charity, or mentoring someone younger, or a new pupil. Doing so reminds them that other people are relying on them and that their behaviour will impact upon that person.

A second turning point came at secondary school when I was lucky enough to start playing rugby league, the dominant sport in Warrington. It didn't feel lucky at the time as I only joined the rugby team because I didn't make it into the town's football team. I was a mad football fan as a kid and a good player too, so it took me by surprise when I didn't make the team. Disappointed, I was encouraged to take up rugby, which is where I met Mr Harrison: a true gentleman but an absolute disciplinarian.

He made us fold our shirts in a particular format. Pull our socks up a certain way. We had to learn to take knocks and keep our cool. In rugby you can have people punching you in the face as you're laying on the ground and you've got to learn to take it.

If looking after the dog was motivating because I found it easy, rugby was motivating because I found it really hard. I was way behind the others in terms of skills when I started. Way, way behind. Everyone else had been playing for years and watching games with their parents, while I had been busy playing football and watching Everton on the telly.

Aged 13, I therefore started getting up each day at 6am to watch video recordings of rugby games from the weekend. I would memorise tactical plays. I would try and figure out what the best players did and mimic it. Later in my career, I would be fortunate enough to meet players like Ellery Hanley and Sean Edwards, guys who were top of their field at that time and who I watched zooming across the telly in the early hours of each school day.

Over time, the dedicated practice paid off. I started beating the other kids who were once way ahead of me. I could outsmart them, run faster, go for longer. It was then that I realised that hard work matters. I couldn't always beat other people with innate talent, but with the determination and energy to work, work, work, then I could still win.

It started to occur to me that if I could work hard and get better at a sport, then maybe I could do the same thing with my studies. By the time I hit year 9 (age 13), I was studying harder and it was starting to pay off. I was never a mega-brain and work was still difficult, but my behaviour came under control and I started to get decent enough grades.

I'll also admit that it wasn't just my hard work that helped achieve this, thanks also must go to Mr Morgan, my head of year. Exams make me really, really nervous. I'll often space out in them and panic. But whenever I did, Mr Morgan would come over and encourage me. That gave me a lot of confidence and saved me on more than one occasion.

I worry sometimes about our exams system today. Not every kid has a Mr Morgan, keeping his eye on them. But what good would it have done for me to fail those exams? If I had, it's highly unlikely I'd have gone on to teach and help as many pupils as I have.

It's funny, given how things have turned out, to think back to our options evenings at school. I remember when Ross went to his options evening with our parents all the teachers wanted him to do their subject. When I went they just said, 'we think it would be better if Drew did something else.' It makes me a bit annoyed, really. Why were they so quick to give up on me? Even my parents, who were always enormously supportive, helped arrange an alternative vocational course for me after 16 as they thought I was going to fail my GCSEs and wanted to make sure that if I couldn't get on to do A-levels I had somewhere to go.

Luckily, things didn't come to that. And, as it turned out, this naughty boy would eventually prove that hard work, commitment and dedication pays off.

Chapter 2 –
A band of brothers

'In the fear and alarm you did not desert me, my brothers in arms' – Dire Straits

The producers of the *Educating Greater Manchester* TV series seemed very taken with the idea of three brothers working together in the same school. Given how different we are, it's certainly surprising that we all ended up there. (And in very different jobs, too). But we've always been quite close. In fact, at one point we were nearly Britain's answer to the Von Trapp family.

If you'd met me and Ben when we were under the age of 15, you'd have thought the most likely way we Povey brothers would have ended up working together was in sport. Both Ben and I are keen Everton fans. Our dad was a supporter and we grew up watching football on television with him. I was football mad. I loved playing it, I loved watching it. I had Everton-themed everything. Bright blue pendants hung on my wall, an Everton haversack on my back as I went to school. It didn't matter how ill-fitting or old the item: if it was Everton, I wanted it.

Ben was also into football and over the years we slowly took over our mum and dad's back garden with our makeshift 'Wembley' pitch. We did that standard childhood thing of imagining a victory in the dying minutes of a game and would spend hours out there practising.

Ross was less keen on both football and rugby. He would be in the house, reading, or figuring out how something worked. Not because he was unfit. He really liked skateboarding, and would hang around with his mates, looking all teenage-y and melodramatic while Ben and I were skidding on our knees celebrating final-minute goals.

It was, however, music that brought us together. And for that we have to blame Ross.

Back in the 1980s, Cheshire County Council, who were in charge of our primary school, were keen on giving everyone an instrument. In junior school, Ross was handed a guitar – and the rest of us have been reaping the benefits, or perhaps regretting that day, ever since! He practised endlessly, while we careered around the garden. Ross is also very lucky in being able to sing perfect harmonies without even trying. From an early age he could just sing alternative parts, and make other people sound much better than they might on their own. I'm a big believer in practice and the '10,000-hour effect', which says that you need to put in that much time to master a particular skill. But, sometimes, a kid is just a freak of nature at something. They just have innate talent. Ross was a natural with music from the start, and then the hours of practice on top meant that he ended up being really, really great.

I was also pretty good at singing and Ben was too. None of us can quite remember when we first sang together, but it was more than likely at the church we attended every weekend with our parents.

At some point, Ross was playing the guitar and I got up to join him. He was playing an Extreme song, with me singing lead vocals. Then, because he could sing automatic harmonies, Ross joined in, and it sounded really great. The audience loved it and people started saying we should make a band. A band of brothers? Who doesn't like that idea!?

First we played at church, then some other events, and gradually it became quite the thing. We called ourselves 'RossAndrew' which was a riff on the fact that my full name is Andrew so when you said the name out loud it sounded like Ross and Drew, but also RossAndrew (one word). To be honest, it was a bad pun even when you said it out loud. Seeing it written down is even worse!

Our songs of choice were hard rock. Ross was well into AC/DC and Status Quo, which is all well and good but when you're playing the RAF Wings Club in Knutsford and your audience is mostly in their seventies this wouldn't always go down so well. To test the waters, we'd play a small soundcheck at the beginning and wait for some reaction. I remember once the secretary of the club high-tailing it across the dancefloor and shouting, 'You can't be playing that muck in here, they'll be up in arms.'

It was the 1990s by this time and line dancing was all the rage. We would ask if people had any requests and inevitably you'd hear a grandma necking a Bells Whisky shouting, 'Do yous not have anything we can line dance to?' Luckily, because Ross was a dab hand at just about any style of music, we used to play 'Walk of Life' by Dire Straits, and a couple of other songs, just to keep everyone happy.

Working the clubs was a great way of learning how to handle a scary crowd. I've always been an optimist, so tend to just carry on regardless, which is a very useful skill when it comes to teaching. Ross also loved the music so much that he tended to get swept away with his passion for a song, even if 30 heavy-looking guys in a St Helen's working man's club were about to start knocking lumps out of each other.

Ross's love of music meant he focused on a future career in the music industry from being quite young. While I was still trying not to get thrown out of school, he had already decided the university he wanted to attend. His goal was studying for a degree in music at the University of Salford, for which he needed two A-levels, including music, and his guitar skills needed to be well beyond Level Eight – the top guitar qualification.

At the start of year 11 Ross went in to meet Mrs Anderton, his head of year, at Bridgewater High School (which we all attended). She was expecting to have a 15-minute career chat with him but he confidently stated that he knew which university course he wanted to take and what he needed to do to get there, along with his full choices for A-levels. She was astonished. She had never come across a student who knew so resolutely what they wanted to do and had been so thorough in researching it.

Still, good intentions don't always make for good outcomes. The Salford course had tough competition for entry. At the time, over 2,000 people applied each year and only 30 got in. He would need to ace his auditions *and* do well in all his exams.

But, for the first time in his school career, Ross struggled. He had chosen theatre studies, music and biology as his three A-levels. But for some reason the content of his biology lesson just wasn't going in. He couldn't remember all the things he needed to remember. Over the year his grades were going down and down.

In an unprecedented move he went to Mrs Anderton and asked if he could drop an A-level. She was appalled. Bridgewater High School was, and still is, a top-notch school with great academic results. It was unheard of that someone would drop an A-level. In today's climate, with published league tables and pressure on heads to get as many exam grades for each child as possible, I suspect it would definitely not be allowed. But Mrs Anderton remembered how grown-up Ross had been about his dream, and how passionate and serious about his music career he was. He only really needed the two A-levels, and he could use the rest of the time to work on his guitar. In a move that likely changed the course of his life she let him drop the A-level. And, because he's Ross, he worked his socks off on the remaining two, plus his guitar.

The only remaining hurdle was the audition (which he passed with flying colours). As I said before, I'm a big believer in the importance of practice and hard work. You can't wait around and rely on other people, you have to get on and do things for yourself. However, the support of parents shouldn't be underestimated, and the way our mum and dad supported all of us is a key part of how we've turned out. The genius of giving me Carrie, the black Labrador, in order to teach me responsibility, is a classic example. With Ross, our parents' unwavering support for his music is another great example. Mum would make him do his piano practice and dad spent hours helping him buy and set up guitars.

If anyone had told Ross at that point that he would become a teacher, I think he would have laughed in their face.

'Because brothers don't let each other wander in the dark alone' – Jolene Perry

For a while it looked like Ross was going to move to Salford in order to go to university but, as luck would have it, students had to live further than 20 miles away to be eligible for student accommodation. Stockton Heath, where we lived, was 19 miles away! So Ross was stuck with us at home, though he didn't seem too worried, in part because we were doing well with the band.

The other reason he was happy to stay at home was that, on his first night at university, one of his friends, Frank, was held up at knifepoint at a cash machine. The gang made Frank take his full day's allowance of cash out of the machine before marching him home, ransacking his house, and holding him until midnight, at which point the bank reset, and they took him back out to get another load of money from the cash machine. That was our family's first real experience of Salford and it's a shame that it's not a better one given how much we now love the place. Still, it shows that Salford is not some sleepy idyll on the outskirts of Manchester. It has always been its own city with its own serious challenges.

Around this time, Ben decided to get in on our music act too. I remember at one gig in Blackpool he put on some puppetry using Tom and Jerry dolls which went down a storm. After that, we would let him perform with us more often.

At the start, however, Ben was our roadie, even though he was only about 14. If Ross is the clever one, and I was the naughty one, then Ben was the freakishly strong one. He's much bigger than me in size, and he was much stronger than Ross and me, even when he was a teenager.

Ben would help us load our speakers and instruments into the little white van we used for transporting equipment between gigs. Unfortunately the van only had two seats upfront. A grill separated the front section, with the seats, from the back section, where we loaded up the equipment. Looking back now I cringe over this but we used to pile the van up with our equipment until there was only a 25-centimetre gap at the top of the van. Then, we'd hoist Ben up so he could lie spread-eagled like a squashed bat across the top of the speakers. Ross and I would then get into the front seats and drive to our gig with Ben clinging on for dear life, inches from the ceiling. Thinking about it now, it's so dangerous. If we'd flipped the car, Ben would have been killed instantly. But at the time we thought it was funny. As we were driving down the road, we'd slam on the brakes so that Ben slid forward and hit his face on the grill. 'We're going to turn you into a Peperami,' we used to say to him, laughing.

Mum did not see the funny side. She saw us one day, loading Ben into his position like a piece of bread in a toaster, and told us we had to stop. Of course, our solution was to change the shape of the equipment and instead squash Ben into a gap at the back of the van which, when I think about it, wasn't much better, as if someone had run into the back of us, it would have still killed him.

We certainly weren't trying to be dangerous but it shows how easy it is when you're young not to see the implications of your behaviour. Even though we were a close set of brothers, and cared for each other, we just didn't see the danger of what we were doing. Young brains are not always good at assessing risk.

We kept the band going for years although we later changed our name from 'Ross and Drew' to 'Against Time'. This was better for including Ben, and it was also a slightly less rubbish name.

We even carried on with the band when Ross moved to London after finishing his degree at Salford. The move was a big change for him, but he was focused on becoming a musician and felt that being in the capital city would make it easier for him to work in studios with big artists. In the week he lived with our uncle in north London, then at the weekend he would come back, as he was doing a master's at Salford University on the Friday, and then we'd gig together over the weekend before he went back to London.

By this point the band was getting successful. We had agents, cruise ship offers, more bookings than we could handle. We even had professional backing tracks. We were definitely rustier than some acts on the cabaret circuit at the time – though that could be good depending on the type of club you were in – but there was a definite sense that the Povey Brother Band would become a professional thing. Just imagine it: us, on stage, every night. It was the stuff dreams were made of!

Then, as so often happens in life, fate intervened. The world wasn't ready for a Povey music sensation. Instead it wanted to make a teacher out of freakishly nerdy Ross after all.

Chapter 3 –
The unusual route of Ross

'If at first you don't succeed try, try and then try something different'

Not many stories about life-changing moments take place at an IT helpdesk, but that's where Ross was when he was offered his first teaching job.

Having been in London for a few months trying to make it as a session musician he took a temporary job at the University of North London as it was then called (now the London Metropolitan University). Ross is great at figuring out how things work, so his technology skills got him a position on the IT support desk, mostly resurrecting lost copies of dissertations which were saved, at the time, on flimsy 3.5-inch floppy disks that had a habit of corrupting just as a deadline approached. The helpdesk had a wonderful piece of software that reversed the problem but not everyone could use it. Ross had a magical way with it, and so quickly became famed as the man who could save your lost work.

One day the head of the university's newly established music department appeared at the desk to inquire about his services. 'So is this your main job?' she asked. Ross explained that he was actually a musician and was studying song composition, part-time, up at Salford University on the weekend.

The woman was suddenly enthusiastic. 'I can't believe we're having this conversation! We are starting a new music undergraduate degree, and we need someone who is trained in pop music to deliver lectures on its application in modern education – do you think you'd be interested?'

Ross wasn't a qualified teacher, but he'd done some private tutoring and figured (rightly) that lecturing was more lucrative than rescuing broken disks, so he jumped at it. By that September, Ross was a university lecturer – which didn't surprise any of us who knew how clever he was!

He worked as a visiting lecturer for five years at the university. He would give talks about popular music on weekdays before coming home to Stockton Heath to gig with us at weekends. A few years into this he was asked, as a favour, to help our old high school, Bridgewater, with their bid to become a specialist arts college. At that time schools could get more money if they had a specialism. As part of the bid he was offered the role of a musician-in-residence a couple of days a week which led to him becoming the assistant arts director. This layered on the workload even further.

At one point Ross would travel all the way home on a Thursday night, work Friday daytime at Bridgewater, gig Friday night through to Sunday, be back at Bridgewater on Monday, jump the train back to London, lecture Tuesday through Thursday and then start the whole process all over again!

That was when the second life-changing surprise happened. This time it was a slightly more glamorous setting than a helpdesk.

We were doing a gig at a friend's birthday party one night when he started chatting to a woman – Don, short for Donna-Marie – who would soon become his wife. Don is from Boothstown, an area of Greater Manchester near Little Hulton, which was an area that none of us had heard of until that point.

If you think Ross was focused with his work, you should have seen how he was with Don! They met in the February, went on a first date in March, were engaged in August and married by the end of December. On top of all his comings and goings from London too!

The change meant that Ross was now looking to move back home permanently. Bridgewater made him their full-time arts director and he worked at the school, running extra-curricular performing arts clubs and leading on collaborations for a few years. He still wasn't a teacher, however. In fact, it still wasn't on his radar. At the time he was planning to move into arts management full-time, or even just stay at Bridgewater.

Then he got talking to his friend, Rob Devlin, who had introduced him to Donna-Marie in the first place. Rob happened to know of a project to get dedicated teachers to a school called Harrop Fold. The school had been created from the merger of two others and had gone badly wrong. It was now onto its fifth headteacher in five terms and results were on the floor. But, there was a silver lining. Despite all its problems, Harrop Fold School was known for being outstanding at performing arts. If there was going to be a route for it to succeed, maybe it would be through the sorts of projects Ross was running at Bridgewater?

If there's a trait that runs through all of us Poveys it's that we love a challenge. For me, I hate the idea of giving up on people. For Ross, his focus means that when he has a goal, he guns for it.

Ross will also tell you that he felt he couldn't let his friend down – after all, this was the guy who had introduced him to his wife. And even if he would be going to Harrop Fold as an unqualified teacher, it might be possible to change the role to arts management in future. How much harder could teaching classes really be?

'People are like tea bags – you never know how strong they are until you put them in hot water' – Eleanor Roosevelt

The night after Ross's first day at Harrop Fold he called me in a panic. In fact, he called or messaged most days throughout those first two terms. Like so many people before and since, his belief that teaching was going to be a doddle turned out not to be true. Of course, he couldn't know otherwise. He hadn't been trained. He had absolutely no idea how to do a lesson plan. He'd never been shown any behaviour management techniques. Harrop Fold was in such a desperate way that anyone who was warm and breathing, and ready to turn up, was taken in.

He'd also never experienced a school like Harrop. Bridgewater High School has been outstanding forever. The idea that children would purposely want to be difficult to someone they hadn't yet met was not something that even entered his head.

On his first morning at the school, his first lesson was with year 9, notoriously the most difficult year group. Even experienced teachers can struggle with a room of hormonal 13- and 14-year-olds.

Nevertheless, Ross knew this lesson was coming and had prepared well in advance. He had set up the classroom just so. He had prepared notes of what he was going to say.

The assistant head brought the group up from the hall, and lined them up outside the classroom.

Ross noticed they were mostly quiet and subdued. 'This is going to be great,' he thought.

The assistant head looked at him and said, 'thank you sir', raising his eyebrow as the cue for Ross to open the door and get the kids inside and sat down. Duly, the kids went in and quietly sat at their desks. Ross was pretty proud of his crowd control skills.

As the assistant head walked towards the door, ready to leave Ross alone with the pupils for the first time, he turned and gave a small thumbs up. 'Good luck, sir,' he said ominously.

The door shut. Ross was alone.

Because of his lecturing background Ross had put a music stand at the front of the classroom with his notes on them. His plan was to dole out wisdom and have the pupils to make notes. On his desk, he had a CD player and some CDs.

'Hi, I am Mr Povey and I have come from Bridgewater High in Warrington,' he said. 'For our first music lesson this term I thought we would look at the sort of music that will interest you. So I have prepared a lecture on the history of rap music.'

No sooner had those words fallen out of his mouth than one kid, Dale, stood up, turned to face the rest of the class and yelled at the top of his voice, 'Who the FUCK does this dickhead think he is?'

And then he started punching the kid next to him in the side of the head. A brawl ensued. The other students had started crowding around the feuding pair when two girls burst in from the corridor – kicking the door in and then running around the room shouting and shrieking.

As anarchy descended, Ross stood frozen in the midst of it all. For a moment, he stood there and thought to himself, 'What have I done? I've made a massive, massive mistake.'

It didn't get better over the following weeks. As I've already mentioned, the school was onto its fifth headteacher in five terms and unsurprisingly was in a state of chaos. No one believed new rules would be followed up on. Community relations had broken down and gangs were warring to such an extent that a police van would turn up each lunchtime to round up feuding pupils who had spent the morning knocking lumps out of each other, and then march them out, handcuffed, into the van. If this public parade was intended as a warning, then it always fell on deaf ears.

Beyond rampaging kids, the buildings at Harrop Fold were also rotten. Built in the 1950s as a post-war quickie, the construction materials were long past their usable life. No one dared remove posters in case the wall came away with the Blu-Tack. And worse of all for Ross, who has a mortal fear of vermin, the place was rat-infested. Teachers were regularly reporting dead rodents under their desks. Kids gleefully threw around dead mice.

The other teachers didn't help. In the music department the only other teacher was also unqualified and had no idea what to do. Ross soon found the only way he could guarantee some peace was to get the kids to play the *Eastenders* or *Titanic* theme tune on the keyboard. Not being a trained teacher, and without any support, the advice he would read in books or learn from other people didn't make sense. There's no use being told to begin a lesson with a 'starter' if you don't know what one is. (Note for non-teachers: A starter is an activity used at the beginning of a lesson to get kids settled down.)

Ross tried hard to get kids engaged by getting them to start bands and take part in concerts, but lessons remained a muddle of shouting, messing about and general bad behaviour. On the rare occasions that Ross managed to get the kids settled and quiet, he would open his mouth and find nothing coming out as he still hadn't been trained in how to give good explanations.

During those first demoralising months the thing that kept him most sane was messaging, phoning, or meeting up with me. I would try and give him my best advice, but it was hard watching him struggle.

Why would Ross think of asking me what he should do? Well, while Ross was busy getting his music degrees I had, in total amazement to everyone and against the odds, just won a National Teaching Award!

Chapter 4 –
How the naughty boy
became a teacher

'Don't be a prisoner of your past'
'Don't wish for it, work for it'

If Ross becoming a teacher was unlikely, then my chances were a million to one. Not only had I struggled all the way through school, but my passions were sport and music. I did well at rugby league, well enough to later help coach at elite level, and the band was also on the way to becoming professional.

So how does a kid, almost excluded from primary school, and constantly behind in his academic work, grow up to be a teacher? It's all about being a tortoise.

You probably remember the story from school about the hare and the tortoise. Originally it comes from Aesop's Fables, created by the slave Aesop, in Ancient Greece. In the story a quick-moving hare ridicules a slow-moving tortoise, who retaliates by challenging the hare to a race. The hare zooms off but looks back at a certain point to see how far ahead he is. Seeing his substantial lead he decides to have a sleep. By the time the hare wakes up the plucky tortoise, who has determinedly continued, has beaten him to the end of the race. It's a simple lesson: laziness can ruin natural ability; hard work can lead to a win.

I love that story for its messages, but also because I am that tortoise. I didn't have a great time at school. I was almost kicked out. But what I had learned by my teen years was that if I had faith in hard work then while the hare snoozes, I could make the finish line.

I kept that attitude up throughout my A-levels. I had to work hard but I managed to get good enough grades to study sport science, philosophy and theology at the University of Chester, which combined my two favourite school subjects, physical education and religious studies.

I've always loved sport, but my love of religion came when I was at secondary school. For some reason, I could just do it, unlike almost all the other academic subjects. It's because there are no wrong answers. Instead, you have to think differently. You're working out situations and people, rather than facts and figures. In RE you say what you think a person should do and give reasons for that answer. It's the strength of the reasons, rather than the inherent 'rightness' or 'wrongness', that matters for success. For some kids, like me, that's a much less scary approach than facing being told you're wrong. I'd endured so much failure at school, because I struggled with reading and my stammer, that finally being good at something was hugely motivating.

Although I got into university, passing my courses did not come easily. While everyone else was hanging upside down in bars pouring alco-pops down their necks through our university years, I was studying. I did two hours in the university library every single day for three years – not something most people on sports science courses can say. But I had to. I'm simply not as gifted as other people. I have to put the hours in or I'll never keep up.

'There are no shortcuts to any place worth going' – Helen Keller

The hard work paid off, and I received a 2:1.

In my final year I had started to think about teaching. I'd been teaching since I was 15 years old, when I first coached a younger rugby team. Coaching was always something I'd found easy. Even when the kids were difficult. Even if the kid didn't want to listen to anyone. Somehow, I could always get through to them.

There was a major snag in the teaching plan, though. I wanted to become a PE teacher but that year the government said they wouldn't fund any PGCEs in the subject. I was gutted because I couldn't afford the fees on my own, and I didn't want to take out another loan. But at the last minute, I got a reprieve. The government sent a letter saying they would fund PGCEs in that subject after all.

Chuffed to pieces, I put in an application to my university and went down to see the staff in the PE department. When I told them, their faces dropped. 'We'd love you to be a PE teacher. You're the best on our coaching course, Drew. But the course is full: 50 places are gone, and the waiting list is already 50 deep.'

I was crushed. Totally crushed. As I walked out of the PE department, I happened to pass through the education department nearby. An older lady, Carole Fry, who had taught me for philosophy, was wandering along the corridor.

I always liked Carole, she was older than most of the lecturers and slightly eccentric, but she was always patient and took an interest in me.

She looked surprised to see me, given it was so late in the year. 'What are you doing here?' she asked.

I explained how the PE grant was awarded late and now the course was full.

'So no teacher training for me this year,' I said.

'Have you thought about being an RE teacher?' she asked. 'There's still some places on our course.'

I stood there looking at her like she was insane. Because, no, of course I hadn't thought about becoming an RE teacher. I was a rugby-playing sports-loving guy who didn't mind having a chat about ethics in a classroom, but I didn't carry a tambourine and wear sandals. (I realise now that's not actually what everyone in the profession is like, but I was naïve back then.)

'Do I look like a religious studies teacher?' I asked her with disbelief.

She laughed. 'Maybe not, but I think RE could really benefit from someone like you – a young man, interested in sports, who is good with the challenging kids. At least think about it!'

Over the weekend I started thinking, if only to humour Carole, and began questioning if it was really so crazy. I liked RE. It was a subject that connects with kids who otherwise felt academically lost. And if I got my PGCE then I could always teach PE later.

By the Monday morning I decided I had nothing to lose so I rang Carole, went in to see her, and signed myself up to become an RE teacher!

The training year was no problem. I'd had a great mentor for years called Fred Shadwell while I was doing my rugby coaching who helped out greatly. He had dark, weathered skin and a bald head. He had been a PE teacher for years, which had aged him at some point, but now his age seemed to stand still. I used to call him Peter Pan. He was a local teacher in Warrington for over 30 years. One of those guys who had worked his way up through the craft, teaching generations of kids, and really figuring out how people (including me) ticked. He was also a local rugby coach and would talk to me about teaching and my career. He was totally instrumental in helping me become the teacher that I would be, and made my training year much easier. He always called me Povey or another more insulting name, but I won't tell you what that was!

Carole was also very tolerant of me, and I found working with the kids and getting them onside to be a fairly easy thing. I loved finding out what pupils thought about issues – abortion, divorce, God. I used to say to them all the time, 'Don't tell me what your family think, or your mates think, tell me what YOU think.'

It's the same technique I use with kids who misbehave. There's nothing more illuminating than asking a kid why they did something. They'll often start by saying 'I don't know' but when you start peeling back the layers – did they think their actions were funny, were they trying to get someone off their back, was it about gaining mates? – then you can really start to see people. That's the thing that connects in RE for me, it's about people, not just facts or right answers.

'If you chase two rabbits, you will catch neither' (Russian proverb)

If there was one sadness about me getting onto the PGCE course, it's that it stopped me going to join Ross in London and taking the band to the next level. I helped him get onto his master's by singing at his audition but, as we both moved into teaching, it became clear we couldn't keep up with both things.

By the end of the PGCE I was on the Warrington Wolves coaching staff and doing that part-time at a rugby-training school. (For those who don't follow the sport: Warrington play in Britain's highest league.)

One afternoon, someone came in to have a look around our training facility. He asked who I was. The guy showing him around said that I'd been brought in to train the youth sides as I was 'decent with the kids' and 'a trained RE teacher, of all the things'.

'Well bloody hell,' the visitor said. 'I've hit the lottery!' That visitor turned out to be John O'Callahan, the charismatic headteacher of Beamont High, a local secondary school, which was in desperate need of a new RE teacher.

John invited me into Beamont that week and asked me to join the school not just as a teacher, but as head of the religious studies department. I couldn't believe it! Without filling in an application form or going to an interview, I was being offered a serious job and a promotion to boot. I took the offer in a heartbeat, believing that such good luck would never come again.

These days, I know better. Good quality religious studies teachers are about as rare as rocking horse droppings. Plus, he managed to persuade me to be his head of department for no extra pay. So I think he probably got the better end of that deal! Still, I was chuffed to pieces at the time.

From the start I had no problems with the kids at Beamont. I trained the rugby team, which helped, and I learned the ropes of teaching among the brilliant teachers there, many of whom were young and just starting out like me. Very quickly I built a good reputation – helped by my behaviour management skills – and so was put forward for a national teaching award.

I received a letter at school one day to find out I was nominated. I was taken aback as my first thought was that many other people deserved it more than me.

The day the National Teaching Awards' camera crew came to film me at work, I happened to be wearing a pair of very short 1980s rugby shorts. I was probably showing a bit too much leg. It was great for the producers, though. There I was, storming around a classroom in my sports kit while holding up an Islamic carpet.

The morning of the awards ceremony I was told they would show videos on breakfast television. I tuned in with hope in my heart but they didn't show my video and, seeing as I also hadn't been contacted in advance, I predicted I hadn't won. Not surprised by this, I went along to the awards ceremony ready to chat to everyone and soak up the atmosphere. I was totally gobsmacked when they announced my name. And a little concerned. Unfortunately I lost my front tooth a few years earlier in a rugby game and the night before the ceremony I had been munching on a spare rib when it lodged into the meat and popped out. I'd fashioned a make-do fixer from chewing gum and denture cream (the sort older people use). As I walked up to get my award all I could think about was my front tooth wobbling backwards and forwards, and whether it was going to shoot out half-way through my thank-you speech.

Even worse, I couldn't smile for the cameras. Fred Shadwell had come along to the ceremony for support and knew about the tooth. He kept shouting ridiculous comments at me when I was trying to do a closed-mouth smile in front of the cameras, and I kept laughing and then having to close my mouth again.

To be honoured like that was a great feeling, though. It gave me more confidence – see that tortoise go! And I also got to meet Gordon Burns the TV presenter. We met again recently at a *Krypton Factor* event at Harrop Fold which he kindly came along to. You never know which people you meet will pop up again at some point!

'When something is important enough, you do it even if the odds are not in your favour' – Elon Musk

I was in my fourth year at Beamont when Ross took his job at Harrop. I was excited for him and thought he'd do really well but I remember him phoning me that first day and saying, 'mate, this is impossible.'

I remember his worst days were Mondays and Tuesdays. Wednesdays got better. By Thursday and Friday he had his favourite classes. Most weeks it was a case of trying to help him get over those first few days and have enough strength to carry on until the end of the week.

What I couldn't work out at first was whether it was Ross or the whole school that was the problem. I would get him to try things out and when they wouldn't work it started to become evident that it wasn't just his teaching, there was a bigger problem all across the school.

The biggest lesson I taught him over those months was the critical importance of follow-up. I used to get him to imagine behaviour management with pupils like he was building a wall. Each incident is like a brick in the wall. If there's an issue with that brick then you have to follow up on it. You have to make sure you speak to the child, give a detention, speak to their parent, whatever it is that you have promised to do as a consequence then you have to follow through. 'You have to be militant,' is what I used to say to him. If you let one of the bricks go in behaviour management then the whole wall will collapse.

Another important trick, which I've used a lot as a headteacher, was getting him to reframe things. He would tell me that whole classes were playing up. I'd ask him, 'Is it really a whole class? Or just a few kids?' A lot of the time it would be just five kids causing the problem. So I would get him thinking about the other 20 in the class who were doing the right thing.

A problem with teaching is that you always remember the one kid who is kicking off. Our brains tend to retain negative memories at around two and a half times the rate of positive ones. We feel them more intensely and so they worm their way in. We remember them better and we focus on them more. One of the reasons I wanted to do the *Educating Greater Manchester* series was so that we could have a record of a whole year at the school which shows all sides of what school life is like – the good, the bad, the ugly and the exciting.

Getting Ross to think about the positives was important too. Some of his classes were very difficult. But he was also getting some kids playing in bands, and starting to take their music seriously. You've got to keep in perspective that the small wins become much bigger wins over time.

One of the things he was really proud of was a Christmas concert he pulled together. He was still having trouble in lessons but he'd managed to get a few kids into bands and they were going to showcase their talents. I saw the concert as a good way to see what this place that he had been bending my ear about was really like.

What I saw when I approached was a 1950s run-down building. It was raining, freezing rain, but from the second I arrived I could tell the school had something special. The concert was amazing and it seemed obvious that if these kids, who people were writing off academically and behaviourally, had the discipline to put together such a concert then it must be possible to do much more with them.

The problem was that the brilliance of the concert was contrasted with depths of absolute misery.

The headteacher, Anthony Edkins, showed me around. He had only just taken over at the school and was commuting from Brighton each week. But he, like Ross and me, felt there was great potential in the school. 'The problem is that the teachers and the kids don't believe it can change,' he said. In their minds, the community had written the school off as a lost cause. Who could blame them after so many years of misery?

All I could think was that it must be awful to be given up on so easily. I knew how horrible that felt.

During my trip I saw kids tearing round without a care for anyone, and teachers letting them do it. That was a real spark of a moment. I wanted to get involved. I wanted to roll my sleeves up and start straightaway.

Ross had been a major coup for the school in terms of teaching, and he was barely even qualified and able to get the kids to sit down. I knew I had to get involved.

The thought of giving up on a place like this didn't sit well with me. Not at all. I couldn't bear the idea that other people didn't care. To this day, the thing that bothers me most is when people don't care enough about the school. That doesn't happen in our local community, they've been brilliant. But the way politicians will focus on their hobby horses and not care about all pupils equally makes me as mad as I was that day watching the kids tear around the corridors without shame. I just knew that we had to make it better.

So the decision to take a job at Harrop was easy. Anthony offered me any position I wanted, and we agreed I would go in as a senior teacher with responsibility for behaviour. Although it was a serious promotion, and a significantly more challenging job, I hardly took a pay rise. I knew the school was struggling and I've never been motivated by money. I asked for an extra grand to cover my travel costs (although my petrol ended up costing a lot more than that anyway).

***

The night before I was due to start at Harrop was at the end of the long Easter holidays in 2005. We'd both had two weeks off. I was ready and primed and knew exactly what I was going to do on my first day to get a grip on behaviour.

At home, Ross was more concerned. He didn't tell me at the time but when he was chatting to his wife, Don, he said that he was worried he'd stitched me up.

'What if he can't handle it?' he said. 'What if I've caused him to leave a job he loves and he struggles just as much as me?'

Strong in her faith in me, Don looked at Ross and said, 'Don't worry, Drew can handle it.'

But neither of them had any idea what I was planning to do on my first day.

Chapter 5 –
The hard lads

'A leader is one who knows the way, goes the way and shows the way' – John C Maxwell

It was the first morning of term as I headed towards the yard on the upper site at Harrop Fold: a concrete jungle, right in the guts of the local housing estate. My mission was simple. I was looking for the hardest lads in the school.

In the yard, the kids were hanging out in groups.

'Who's the hardest lad in the school?' I asked a group of year 11s stood moodily to one side.

'Who wants to know?' one said.

'I want to know. Who's the hardest lad in the school?'

My new friend nodded over to another group, playing football on the yard. 'He is.'

I looked over at the kid in question. Tall, strong-looking, a classic hard lad.

And so I called over to him: 'Hey! Who's the hardest lad in the school? Is it you?'

'What's it to you?' he replied.

'I just want to know who the hardest lad is. Is it you?'

'No,' he blurted, pausing to look me up and down. 'It's those guys.'

As I walked over to yet another group, the tall boy followed. I was starting to get quite a crowd. Why was some idiot stranger in his 20s walking around the schoolyard and trying to single out the tough lads?

'Who's the hardest lad in the school?' I asked this third lot.

'Why do you want to know?' the toughest-looking one asked.

The rest were now craning to hear my response.

I walked up to him. 'Because I'm Mr Povey, and I teach here now, and I want the hardest lads in the school to come to the gym tomorrow morning at breaktime.'

'Why?'

'Does it matter? You're either the hardest lads or you're not. And I'm going to be in the gym tomorrow at breaktime, and I want to see the hardest lads in there.'

'Are you going to fight us, sir?' they asked as I walked away.

I didn't answer.

Overnight, the word spread. I think most of them thought I was going to try to knock them out. (Obviously, I wasn't!)

If you can imagine a gym from a cheesy 1980s high school movie, then you're in the right ballpark for what that next morning looked like. The school gym was like nothing I'd ever seen. It had a scabby felt floor, torn up all over the place. The walls were dingy and dark. As morning lessons finished, the kids started coming in. It was a right motley crew that filtered in. I'd never seen so much jewellery in one gym. Kids with moustaches, some as tall as houses, others who looked like they'd never smiled.

This was exactly the group that I wanted.

On my own, I stood up and said, 'Right boys, thanks for coming.'

They all looked at me, waiting for it to kick off.

'So you're the hard lads are you?'

Silence.

'Come on. Are you at least the lads everyone thinks are the hard lads?'

Murmurs of yes started.

'I'm hard, sir,' said one.

'I've never lost a fight,' said another.

'Good, this is good,' I said. 'Because I'm looking for the hardest lads in the school to build a rugby league team. The roughest, toughest, nastiest, but fairest, rugby league team any school has ever had.'

I kept on. 'But I don't want soft lads. If you have to punch people, if you can't handle yourself and you have to lash out, if you find you have to swear when you get upset, then you can walk right out the door now. Because, one, you're not playing in this team, and two, that means you're not actually that hard. Hard lads can handle themselves. So if you're a soft lad, you might as well walk out now as you'll not get in this team and you'll be wasting my time and yours.'

I held my breath and watched them intently. A few of the boys looked at one another.

All of them stayed.

What I didn't know at the time, and would go on to learn later, was that a couple of the lads were already on the verge of signing for Salford Reds, a top-flight rugby league team – what a huge advantage!

The following night we had our first rugby practice. Some of the guys were large and thought of themselves as real hard lads. I wasn't the tallest guy in the room, so a few cockily thought they could knock me down. But I was used to playing at a decent level and these were 15-year-olds. It didn't matter their size, I ran rings around them.

'This guy is well sound,' I remember hearing one kid say and all the others agreed. Respect from the hard lads was won.

Getting them onside cascaded to the whole school. When a year 9 misbehaved, one of the older boys they feared would say, 'eh, you have to behave because Mr Povey is sound.' After that, they'd soon back down.

'With great power, comes great responsibility' – Spiderman

At this point it's worth explaining a few things. First, I don't think this approach is the only way to win over the respect of kids. I've seen many leaders approach things differently. My personal assistant, Julie, is always dealing with the challenging pupils who are sent to see me. She has her own approach. Likewise, Ross had to find his own path with the students – which he did in a very different way to me.

Second, I'd had practice dealing with difficult people and had honed this sort of technique. Not just in rugby league, but also in my work as a doorman, years earlier.

Back when I was at university I had trained at a place called O'Malley's gym. Half the guys there worked the nightclubs in Warrington. At the time it was a rowdy town, with Fridays and Saturdays seriously frantic.

My mate Griff and I signed up to become doormen too, but were chuffed to pieces when we dodged the main town and were instead dispatched to The Village Hotel – a fancy looking pub on a nearby retail park. It's the sort of place you go for a works knees up at Christmas or your uncle's 40th birthday. So we thought, at least. The night before we started, two officers from a nearby prison were hospitalised in there. Worse still, on our first night, a party was booked for a massive gang of glass workers renowned for being banned from every other local pub.

Griff was worried. Even though he was the size of a house, he seemed bothered. 'If this kicks off, I'm going to the bathroom,' he said.

'Look mate, we're just going to have to deal with it,' I said.

'You can deal with it,' he said, 'Bathroom for me.'

As the glasswork guys approached the door I could see they were massive. They're used to hauling heavy material in high temperatures, there was no way we could take them down if things kicked off.

But, if there is one thing I had learnt as a youngster, it's that people just need to be treated nicely. If you start treating people like they're bad apples, then they start behaving that way. If you're polite to people, it can catch them off guard.

I scanned the room for the biggest lad I could see amongst the crowd, and spotted a mountain of a man called Dave, standing at the bar with a pint in his hand.

I made my way over to Dave. He could fill a door frame. In my head I was thinking 'oh no' but, out loud, I managed to say, 'Hiya guys, how are you doing this evening?'

'We're alright,' grunted Dave.

'Brilliant,' I said. 'Well, I just wanted to introduce myself. I'm Drew, I'll be your doorman this evening, and I want you guys to have a good night so if there's any problems, just come over and see me and I'll sort you out.'

Dave looked at my outstretched hand for a second, and then shook it.

'If there's any problems at all on our side, should I come and get you Dave?'

Dave nodded. 'Yup, sound.'

A few hours later one of their guys got really drunk and grabbed the bottom of a waitress. She came over wanting him to leave. I went over and spoke to Dave.

'We've got a problem,' I said.

True to his word, Dave sorted him out. He found the perpetrator, stuck him in the other bar with a coffee and only let him back in when he'd sobered up and was ready to say sorry. We never had a spot of trouble after that.

For the rest of the time Griff and I were on the doors we always did the same thing. Identify the hardest-looking bloke in the crowd, introduce yourself, use him as a lynchpin. We never had any problems and we weren't great bouncers to be honest, but it proved that being nice would get us further than being difficult, and that getting the troublemakers onside is a damn good strategy.

To this day I am someone who is not afraid to face up to students who are being lairy. I would never hurt a child but I will tell them off. Fiercely, too. I'll shout or slam my hand against a desk if I think that's what it takes to get their attention. I'm not stern because I want to bully kids but because, sometimes, there are kids who will do really bad things – genuinely, very dark and dangerous things – and when I speak with them it's got to be forceful or it won't break the surface.

In the first episode of *Educating Greater Manchester* you will have seen this when some of the pupils were caught on camera drawing rude pictures in the dirt on the back of a white van. Although I saw the funny side beforehand – the programme shows me saying this in the doorway of Ross's office – I still had to be serious when I went in and spoke to the pupils.

The reason I know a certain level of strictness is needed is because I needed someone who could bring me down a peg or two. What worked for me was someone who could do a disappointed, quiet face. When my mum does that, to this day, it breaks me. For other kids, usually big tall lads who walk around at home doing what they want, a quiet disappointed face will mean nothing. They have seen it too many times and there's never been a consequence so it doesn't work. They need someone who can cut through and show that their behaviour is serious. Sometimes that means shouting and showing your anger on your face.

Being strict with a kid can make them cry. A big hard lad who is knocking his mum about at home and carrying on in his lessons is sometimes shocked when he sees angry behaviour from someone else. The shock can be scary. It means the defences they have created to keep people at bay won't always work, and so they cry.

The crucial thing is that every kid I shout at knows I would do anything for them. I want them to know that I care about them. The whole reason why I get so animated and harsh with them is precisely because I care so much. I never, ever leave that sort of conversation without making it clear that I care about them. That's how we have got behaviour under control at Harrop

The reason the hard lads responded wasn't just because I fronted up to them. It was because I was showing up for them week after week at rugby practice. I learned their names, and listened to them. I talked to them about nutrition, and what they wanted to achieve in the future. It's the part where you finally get them to believe that you care which is what really makes all the difference.

I also believe the area needs teachers, particularly a headteacher, with a reputation for taking no nonsense. People in the community have had a raw deal over the years. There has been very little regeneration, there aren't many good employment opportunities, and parents are often living in uncertain situations when it comes to money, housing, and so on. Parents are therefore used to having to fight when they want things. If the head can be pushed over, they will push. Not because they're bad people, but because they care about their kids and want to defend them. So I have to be the person who pulls them up and says, 'Sorry, this behaviour from your child is just wrong. It's wrong. And we are not going to put up with it, and you are going to work with us to sort it out.'

Likewise, many of the boys we get at Harrop Fold are the 'man of the house'. They rule the roost at home. Sometimes they're the eldest lad and they're expected to take on responsibility for younger siblings, or to be a support for their parents. On the outside they put on an act to deal with it all. The swagger in their walk, the way they swear to keep people at arm's length. But it's scary to deal with all that stuff when you're a 15-year old boy. And I know what that's like. When I couldn't read well at primary school it was much easier to act confident, make everyone laugh and stick my fingers in blancmanges than it was to show the vulnerability.

Kids need to understand, however, that if they carry on their biggest problem is not going to be me shouting at them. It's going to be someone with a glass in their hand smashing it into their face or worse.

There's a brilliant book by Steven Peters, a sports psychiatrist, called *The Chimp Paradox* which explains how each of us has an inner monkey. The monkey represents the parts of our brain that goes back to our ancestors who were more like chimps than today's humans. This bit of our brain feeds on gut and instinct: it makes snap judgments, it sees things in black and white. The paradox is that we need the monkey brain because it matters for survival; it helps us jump out of the way of cars or run away from danger. But if we don't learn to manage the monkey – if everything the monkey says, we do – then it will ruin our lives. We live our lives reacting to things.

Getting the hard lads into rugby helped channel this energy. It has a huge amount of discipline to it as a sport. It gets all the parts of the body and brain going, but you also have to be disciplined to win – for the simple reason that you can't spend every five minutes complaining that something in life isn't going your way. People will give you a knock and you have to carry on anyway.

We have a couple of former rugby players working at the school who have trained up to become brilliant qualified teachers. It means there are people on staff who have a different approach dealing with fights and aggressive behaviour. These guys have a good relationship with the kids and will talk to them about their health. A lot of our male students are quite obsessed with muscles and getting fit. They see it as a way to protect themselves, but it means that we can teach them about discipline.

It takes loads of willpower to get up every morning and do a workout. I get up every day at one minute to five and haven't missed a morning of training in over 10 years. So we talk to them about that. Plus about diet, exercise, and supplements. We tell them it's a discipline, but if you embrace a discipline then the compound effects in years to come will make you a better person.

If anyone thinks that's pie-in-the-sky thinking and going to the gym doesn't make much difference academically, it's worth remembering that Professor Dylan Wiliam, who created all the Assessment for Learning strategies in schools which have been wildly successful over the past two decades, was turned around at school by a weight-lifting coach who had exactly this attitude. You simply never know which kid will benefit from the discipline of sport, or how.

Still, this isn't the only approach to getting pupils onside. Consistency and being yourself are the real key. My parents were great for that. Everyone needs to have someone in their corner. These days, mine is my wife. I get so nervous when I have to give talks. I practice and practice. I've never given a talk without putting in at least 100 hours of practice first. But I know that my wife, Vicki, will support me no matter what. That's what we all need to know: that no matter what we say or do, someone is going to be there for us.

Kids who don't have someone to depend on face a very scary world and so they kick off. They challenge. They test. They try to see if anyone does care or if the person who they think is a fake is going to shut down and run for the hills as soon as things get difficult.

'Be yourself, everyone else is already taken' – Oscar Wilde

All of which brings us back to Ross. If you ask him what the worst day was in his first year at Harrop Fold, he can't remember. Every day was a worst day. The school was unmanageable, dangerous, chaotic. The kids were acting in a belligerent way and he couldn't control it.

After months of listening to his war stories, it was time to see him in action. The lesson was supposed to be about key signatures, something about the key of G major, but the kids were just shouting over him. I helped get them settled with the help of one of the naughtiest kids, Joe, who told the rest to be quiet ('ssshhh, Mr Povey is here') but even then Ross struggled. His explanations were dry, nothing seemed to be coming out right. I couldn't follow what was going on. It was like he was having a panic attack in front of my eyes.

As the kids fizzled out of the class and into the corridor I wasn't quite sure what I'd witnessed.

Dazed, I asked Ross, 'What did I just see?'

'I know,' said Ross, 'it's terrible isn't it.'

I looked at him confused. 'Yes, but … seriously, who were you?'

'What do you mean?'

'Mate, the one thing they are going to sniff out straightaway is when you are not being yourself. I don't know who that person is that you were just pretending to be but, seriously Ross, you've got to be yourself, because they are making mincemeat out of you.

'Where's your confidence? Where's the wacky, brainy musician we all know and love? I know I'm your brother but seriously: lose the act.'

Ross looked like I'd hit him for a moment and then said, 'I'm not acting Drew, I'm trying to do my best impression of you.'

I couldn't believe it. My older brother who had always been miles ahead of me academically somehow thought I was the person he needed to be in this situation.

'Mate, that's never going to work,' I said, 'You've got to be you.'

In the weeks that followed he took the advice seriously. In all the time he had been at the school he had never played his guitar in lesson for the kids to see how talented he was. He was trying so hard to be someone else that he had forgotten how impressive his own skills were.

He was also used to thinking himself as a university lecturer. They don't whip out guitars half-way through seminars in order to show what they can do. Ross had to unlearn that old way of doing things and re-imagine himself as a teacher. Not imagine that he was me, but re-imagine himself as the teacher that he really was.

Re-imagining is a big part of what we've done at Harrop Fold. It's based on the phrase that was used after the 9/11 towers came down, that same month in which the school opened. Faced with rubble and ruins the architects had to work out what they were going to do. 'Don't rebuild, re-imagine' was the phrase they used. It's such a simple phrase, but it's amazingly powerful.

Ross had to figure out the teacher he was going to be. Our brother Ben, in time, would forge his own Harrop path. As a school, we had to re-imagine ourselves out of the miserable state we were in and into a success.

Chapter 6 – Leadership by wandering about

'We live our lives in line with the stories we tell ourselves'

Let's be clear, when I arrived at Harrop Fold, the headteacher, Anthony Edkins, was doing a fantastic job of getting the place back into shape. But the staff didn't believe things could be turned around and the kids didn't believe that teachers were going to stick it out or care about them. When you've had five headteachers in five terms, that's understandable. Although I had quickly got the hard lads on side, getting everyone to buy into my big-picture vision was going to be more complicated.

Through my years in sports coaching, I have become really interested in leadership theories. Weirdly, religious education started it. It was that fascination with why people make the decisions they do. That was compounded when I got more into sport, and every morning when I do my workouts I listen to leadership audiobooks.

One of the biggest differences between leadership theory now versus the 1980s is that it used to be focused on 'management'. The idea was that if you got the structures and processes in an organisation aligned, then everything would be okay. Researchers in the 1990s realised this wasn't always the case. Actually, the people in an organisation matter a great deal.

However, there's a useful story from one of the 1980s management case studies. Hewlett Packard, famous for printers and photocopiers, had a sign on the wall in its offices in Palo Alto out in California. It read 'MBWA', which stood for 'Management By Wandering About'. Its leaders believed that if managers wandered about in an unstructured and unplanned manner, checking on employees' situations and machines, then issues were more likely to be picked up and resolved. At the time, it was a revolutionary idea. The randomness and spontaneity of the tours around the organisation meant people didn't cover things up when they knew the boss was on the way, or try to put on a show. Instead they knew that supportive managers might come in at any time, see how they were doing, listen to them and help them improve things.

Ultimately, the idea is one of 'high touch leadership', where leaders are very visible and staff feel that they can approach them to have a conversation. Working in this way builds relationships and encourages others within the organisation to get out and about themselves, understanding the challenges of teams they are managing. Doing so brings greater empathy with staff, which enables the organisation to work more effectively.

In Japan they have a similar concept. It's called the Gemba walk and used by Toyota. Gemba is the Japanese word for 'real place' and it's all about getting a true sense of what is going on in an organisation by having real conversations with people on the ground. The difference with a Gemba walk is that they have a specific focus. So you might set off knowing that you are going to look for all the examples of bad fire safety, or try and find all the most positive things happening in the workplace that day. What matters most is that over time you are uncovering a true picture.

Leading from a distance was never going to be an option for Harrop Fold. An organisation in crisis needs to see the leader at all times. I figured that by going around the school every day, in a very visible way, I could let the students know that I was always going to see them at least once. It was a clear message that if there were any issues then I would know about them and deal with them and, likewise, be there to celebrate any successes.

I called the process 'touring' and I'm proud to say that in the past 12 years I've only missed 48 daily tours out of a possible 7,000 – with a quarter of those in the past year, as I've increasingly been working with external organisations to resolve the Harrop Fold debt. During my first 11 years, I missed an average of just over three tours per year.

I'd like to say I had a comprehensive plan when I started and was tracking progress as I went. But, I wasn't. I didn't even truly understand who the tours would impact most strongly. The whole thing was iterative. What I did notice as I went along was that they started affecting every student, every staff member. What was originally me having a wander quickly became 'leadership by wandering about' – my own version of what was happening in Hewlett-Packard, or in the Japanese Gemba walks.

Leadership by wandering about, or LBWA as I call it, makes a difference in all sorts of ways.

I could go into any classroom and ask: 'Are there any problems today, miss?' If a teacher told me that so-and-so had been giving lip, or not getting on with their work, I could speak to the pupil and find out what was going on. Too often people forget to actually talk to teenagers. I'm always asking kids why they did something and then we look at whether that's in accordance with their values. Not the values they pretend to hold to look good in front of their friends, but their actual beliefs.

What I didn't realise at first was how important LBWA was for the staff. At first, many were just grateful to have some back-up and no longer feel like they were dealing with behaviour problems on their own. If you think back to Ross's first lesson with the difficult year 9 group, a big part of the issue was that he felt on his own. The door shut, and when he was confronted with 30 rampaging teenagers he didn't have any back-up. It was just him and his music stand trying to quell a crowd.

As soon as I started my tours, teachers knew someone had their back. Each day they saw a friendly, supportive senior leader at least once. Even if they didn't think of me as friendly to start with (and some of them weren't keen, I'll admit), I persevered. I've never been easily put off by someone frowning or telling me stop doing something – in fact, it often makes me more determined!

If anything, when a teacher was stand-offish, I would be friendlier. 'Hi, I am just sticking my head in to see if there's anything I can do to help. How are the kids getting on today?' Although the trust issues were huge, they gradually saw me as someone who was supportive. Telling people when I saw good things that 'this is great, you're doing a brilliant job' also helped develop that trust.

As I've moved on to become a headteacher it has sometimes been trickier to get across the idea that these tours are about supporting the staff rather than micro-managing. Newly qualified teachers can panic a bit when I walk in. I see them thinking, 'Oh no, why is the headteacher checking up on me!' But monitoring people in a negative way is not what it's about.

'We make a living by what we get, we make a life by what we give' – Winston Churchill

One of the leadership theories I find the most compelling is 'servant leadership'. It's a reasonably old theory, developed by Robert Greenleaf, a philosopher, in the 1970s.

The definition of a servant leader is someone who sees themselves as a 'servant first'. Greenleaf says, 'It begins with the natural feeling that one wants to serve, to serve first.' The different thing they do, compared to others, is that servant leaders 'make sure that other people's highest priority needs are being served'. They are worrying about whether teachers have equipment, and kids have enough food. They're not worrying about impressing the next inspector who comes in just to make sure they can puff up their own CV.

Hence, when I go into a newly qualified teacher's classroom, it's not because I'm trying to catch them out or performance manage them. Tours are about supporting the mission of the school. Very quickly people understand that if there's an issue in the classroom or if there's an issue with a student, we are there to get them help, not kick them when they're down.

I learned something else, one of the most important things, about LBWA from a visitor. A woman studying for her national professional qualification in headship came to look at the tours. She asked why we did them.

I gave my usual answer. 'It's great to connect with the students, it keeps you in touch, it builds relationships with staff and teams. It's not a performance management tool, it's about leading, it's about people, it's about the direction of travel, it's about the strategy of the organisation.'

When she finished writing her report, she told us we had underestimated the impact the touring had on students. When she spoke to the children they said it had helped raise their standards. 'We want to make Mr Povey proud when he comes into our classroom. We want to show off and show that we're a great class and we want to get better,' they told her.

This had completely missed me. I understood that tours helped teachers to up their game, and that dealing with issues improved connections with students and staff. But the pride angle, and students wanting to have their headteacher be proud of them, had bypassed me.

These days, there's not just me doing tours. Other staff members do them as well. Some book in to do them with me as part of their own training and development. Teachers can easily become isolated: only seeing their own classroom, corridor, or pupils. On tours they see all the different areas of the school. One pupil who is a nightmare in geography might be flying in maths. We discuss that. Why is their behaviour inconsistent from one lesson to the next? What is going on that's working differently in that class? I wish my primary school teachers had toured to see what Mrs Firth was doing to sort out my behaviour. It might have saved us all some heartache!

The second thing we are doing now is making sure that tours are about more than just behaviour. Like with the Gemba walks, we sometimes wander with a focus. I'll try and find out the best things that are happening so we can share them at a staff meeting. Or maybe we'll focus on teaching and learning. I've also changed the questions I ask on tour. I might ask staff how things are going, but also ask the students too – after all, they want to be involved and to give their opinions too.

When there are difficulties with a class (and our teachers are very honest about this) I ask, 'Who in here feels they have let themselves down today?' Being direct like that challenges the students to reflect and self-evaluate, and they usually do own up. Visiting leaders from other organisations often comment that they are surprised by the honesty of our staff and students. Both groups can talk about the journey they took to get here and feel real pride in what they've achieved.

School leaders should get comfortable with listening to criticism from these groups too. Students have every right to have their voices heard. They are people contributing to the success of Harrop Fold as much as the teachers and leaders are.

Which brings me to the second thing that was instrumental in getting the pupils onside in those first few rocky months at Harrop.

On this particular day, when we were still battling the serious behaviour issues, I was asked to attend a senior leaders meeting. The team was discussing how the pupils were frequently breaking safety glass in fire doors in the old buildings. Replacing them was costing £300 a time and the kids were breaking three a day. It was costing the school the best part of £1,000 a day.

I couldn't believe it. That's a huge amount of money for what was silly misbehaviour, not to mention dangerous. As I walked around the school, I started talking with the pupils about it. I would explain both the damage and the costs and say to them: 'This is your school. The money given to the school is for you. Spending it on little pieces of glass isn't a great way to use the money, but it's costing £1,000 a day. A grand a day!'

I came up with an idea which we announced to the whole school.

'Here's an idea,' I said, 'if we don't break any glass panes for two weeks, it will have saved us £10,000. That's great for you and great for the school. Why don't we not break them and spend the money on something else? If you've got any ideas what you want to spend the money on then come and see me.'

Basketball was big at the time so the kids came to me and said, 'We want a basketball court.' I talked with the business manager and the plan was agreed. No broken windows for two weeks and in return we'd build a basketball court.

In the Hollywood version of this story not a single window would be broken, but that wouldn't be true. After going a full week, then a week and a half, and getting all the way to Friday afternoon, they cracked. Well, the glass did. That last afternoon, we had a window broken. It was a tough moment because we didn't want to go back on what we'd said but we'd saved over £9,500 by then and felt it was worth going ahead as long as we communicated why we were going ahead with it.

They got the message, 'If we work together, we can do something pretty fantastic!' It was a significant moment for building trust, and the start of a new relationship between us all. The kids saw it wasn't worth working against us. They could work with us instead.

Building trust with the staff did take longer. It was probably at least 18 months before they were all on-side. One of my first mentors, Fred Shadwell, a teacher at my first school in Warrington, advised, 'The kids are going to do whatever you ask them to, you won't have a problem with the kids. But, you're going to have to work to get the staff with you.' If I went back in time I'd do a fair few things differently, in particular I'd have got everyone talking to each other more. At times we were guilty of dictating things rather than bringing the staff with us.

The one thing I knew was that basic psychology tells you humans want to do something brilliant. You just have to give them the route to making it happen. Not everyone makes the journey all the way to the end; not everyone makes it straightaway. But I had no doubt, not even once, that I could get the kids and the staff on the road towards brilliance with me and Anthony, and I knew I was enough of a persistent person to keep dragging them along that road.

Gradually, results started going in the right direction and school began to feel more stable. Teaching was improving, young people were learning, and the environment was safe. Where there had previously been senior leaders on footballers' salaries who wouldn't take accountability for behaviour, now everyone knew that if you had a problem, help was on the way.

It did require a lot of work from staff too, though. They had to up their game both in teaching terms and in making sure that they followed up on bad behaviour.

In those early months staff would come up to me and moan about how kids were running around the corridors when they were trying to eat their lunch. I would say to them, 'Come out of your classroom and eat your lunch in the corridor then. It's our collective responsibility to look after behaviour. I can't be in eight places at once.'

I challenged the staff to watch the kids, in a professional way, and make sure every pupil knew that every staff member was doing their very best. Being a teacher is not about having an easy life, it's about the kids.

 Unfortunately, not everyone could handle the change. The ones who weren't up for the challenge had to go. I didn't have to do that personally as Anthony, the headteacher, was in charge of that part.

A lot of staff members did wind up leaving in the end. At one point, the school was employing 30 supply teachers a day. Now, thankfully, the turnover is low. On average, only a handful of our teachers move on each year, which is quite an achievement for any school.

'The first step before anyone else in the world believes in it, is that you believe in it' – Will Smith

After five terms of relentless hard work, Harrop Fold finally came out of special measures. People underestimate what that means in a local community like Little Hulton. When things are constantly labelled as 'inadequate', young people in the area start to believe that's all they are worth. Showing progress is enormously motivating.

That said, the inspection report in 2005 which took us out of special measures was far from a slam-dunk success. We were rated as 'satisfactory' – only one grade higher. (Though another way to think of it would be to say that it was also only one step behind 'good'!)

The report hailed Anthony's leadership as outstanding and the school's management did receive a 'good' rating overall. Some achievement, when you consider the state that the place had been in just two months earlier.

The report read: 'The transformation in the school over the last four terms has been remarkable, and there is a strong capacity for further improvement. The school's assessment that leadership and management is satisfactory is too modest a view given the degree and rate of change. A positive ethos for learning has been established.'

Compliments like those were nice to hear. We'd worked tirelessly and knew we were doing the right things but getting that independent stamp of approval made all the difference.

The grade bump also boosted staff morale. From the start Anthony had said we needed to upgrade the conviction of our staff. People had to start believing that our young people could achieve just as well, or better, than kids anywhere else in the country. Not 'as good as', but better. Some of our kids are dealing with all kinds going on in their families – parents going to prison, gangs hanging out in the apartment blocks, shuttling from one family home to the other – and yet, they come to school every day and give it their fullest because they know we care for them and they want to live up to our expectations.

Getting that 'satisfactory' grade allowed people to start believing that they were going to be part of something special. Everybody wants that. We all have a desire to be part of something and to belong.

Almost overnight the mindset of every staff member shifted from being 'we can't do this' to 'we are achieving something people thought was impossible!' Then the community started to catch that belief, then the parents, and soon everything was getting easier.

Three years later, in 2008, when I was still working as a deputy headteacher, we secured another Ofsted 'satisfactory' – this one with even more glowing comments.

It said the leadership was 'forward looking' and had created an ethos that ensures 'students are provided with an orderly environment within which they can learn and make progress'. Compared to 2005 when we were being praised simply for getting kids' anger management under control, this was a leap, even though the grade hadn't changed.

The real icing on the cake was that the first paragraph mentioned how well-regarded the school had grown within the local community. The report added: 'As one [parent] commented, 'The school has improved and gone from strength to strength.'

Don't get me wrong. I wasn't happy because Ofsted was saying these things. The inspector's job is to come in and judge our whole community and all the things we do in a couple of days. It's an incredibly limited, very shallow, system.

My experience of the inspectors themselves has also been mixed. The ones who come to judge us are sometimes years out of the classroom and well behind in their understanding of current issues. In the cases where they've only ever taught in a leafy suburban grammar school, they struggle to understand some of what is going on in a school like ours. So, to be blunt, what Ofsted has to say about our school is not what keeps me awake at night. But hearing that parents think of us highly and that the school has improved? That means everything.

We were also helped in 2008 by moving into a new building instead of struggling on in the rat-infested split site. Finally united under one roof, the school now had better arts and sports facilities.

But it did not come cheap. In total, the new building cost £24m and was paid for via a PFI – short for Private Finance Initiative – which was a type of funding structure developed by New Labour in the 2000s. A lot of people moan about PFIs and they have caused serious problems for schools over the years. As I was to learn when I later took over the headship, there have been some very negative consequences for our budget. But I also know what the building meant to the people of Little Hulton and, at the time, there was simply no other way of getting our hands on that kind of money. Bankers were doling out cash to stick their name on new academies down in London. Many fewer wanted to help a council-run school in the north.

That 2008 inspection report also highlighted something else that had happened in our school over the intervening period. When Ross had arrived at Harrop Fold, the number of exclusions was ludicrous. Kids were being taken out of school by police officers into awaiting vans, and then kept at home for days on end because no one knew what to do with them. The Ofsted report in 2003 describes how more than 130 exclusions had taken place in the preceding *term* alone. That's just 12 weeks. That's almost three kids per day being sent home. Four children were permanently excluded in that time. One every 15 working days. The mind boggles.

By 2005, when the inspectors gave us the first 'satisfactory' rating, they praised the work we were doing to help the kids pastorally, but I was uneasy about something. It's a dirty secret that when results are rapidly improving in schools, many times it is because the most challenging kids are being picked off and sent elsewhere. I see it all the time, even today. Some schools simply won't keep any kid who is at risk of getting lower grades. They rinse them off their registers as soon as possible.

We were not doing this. At Harrop, we were trying hard to keep as many kids as possible, though we were still using temporary exclusions as needed and permanent ones would sometimes follow. Yet, when you think about it, exclusions are ridiculous. Why would sending a kid home to play on their computer or sleep all day lead to a change in their behaviour? If you're excluding more than a hundred kids in one term then it certainly isn't making the change in their behaviour that is needed.

I decided that I wanted us to work towards a 'no exclusions' policy. No matter what. I hated it when teachers gave up on me and I wanted to be able to look parents in the eye and say that I would never, ever give up on their child.

This wasn't something I could tackle on my own, though.

see p76 also

71

Chapter 7 –
Another Povey brother

'People, even more than things, have
to be restored, renewed, revived,
reclaimed, and redeemed; never throw
out anyone' – Audrey Hepburn

Today, at Harrop Fold, we don't exclude any pupil. That was already a target for me in 2007, and I was working towards it with a passion, but we did not yet have the skills, resources or – crucially – the right people to make it possible.

That's when my mind turned to Ben. At school he was a mix between the two of us. Not as naughty as me, not quite as good with the books as Ross. He's a big guy, though, and strong, so he did really well at rugby league and even managed to play a few games for Warrington Wolves. He was also a talented musician and, as I've mentioned before, joined our band for cameos – especially once his Tom and Jerry puppetry took off!

(An interesting aside is that he also never shared a room with me, but instead shared with Ross. I think I was too much trouble for either of them!)

Unlike Ross and I, Ben decided not to go to university. I've no doubt he could have made it if he wanted to, but he was putting all his energy into rugby at the time. Later he took on work with young people in care homes. This meant he was specifically skilled in working with young people who had attachment disorder, which covers a range of behaviours rooted in early neglect, abuse or distressing separations. The maltreatment suffered by the child disrupts the bonds which give infants their sense of safety in the world. Without this sense of safety, as the child grows up they can develop trust issues, a quickness to anger, distortion of emotions, and inappropriate responses to strangers (both overly friendly and unfriendly).

There is some controversy over the extent to which attachment disorder can be diagnosed, and how many children are affected by it, but it is listed in both the ICD-10 and DSM-IV, which are the world's most commonly used official manuals for mental disorder. Even if you're not keen on the idea of a medical-sounding phrase to label behaviours, you only have to spend a few days in a school with a challenging intake to see the sorts of behaviours described in the attachment disorder literature. A few minutes talking to the children, and really understanding what is going on for them, will quickly reveal that in many cases their behaviour is being triggered by all kinds of complex issues and beliefs related to events in their life outside of school.

Imagine, for example, that when you were seven years old, the police had come knocking in the middle of the night. They kicked down the front door, found you barricaded in a bedroom with your parents, one of whom was arrested with a strong use of force and then dragged off to prison with no hope of coming out again. A rare few kids might be unaffected by such events, but most are likely to be traumatised. Their dad is gone, and they may be frightened even to go to sleep at night. The whole family's world may be falling apart around them. Perhaps mum now has to get a job, or two jobs, and the one figure who was at home all day is barely available. The only time the kid gets to see their dad is once every few months – riding a bus for hours to sit opposite him at a visiting desk. And now this boy is the man of the house: expected to be brave, and strong, and start bringing money home soon.

Under such circumstances, the likelihood is that a kid is going to start testing all of the people in their lives. Is every other adult going to disappear on them too? They might be looking at you, as their teacher, and wondering whether you just see them like their dad – as a future criminal who will end up in prison.

The impact on a kid of the whole town knowing their father has been put in prison should also not be underestimated. These are the things that headteachers who hammer challenging students never seem to understand. Kick that kid out, put another negative label on them, and they are not easily going to turn themselves around.

So I mentioned to Anthony that Ben had received this training around attachment disorders. Not because I thought he should give Ben a job, but because I thought he might want to speak to him about it, as that area of psychology was still fairly poorly understood. I thought Ben could maybe come in and train the staff a little.

Anthony was surprised when I told him about Ben. 'How many of you Poveys are there?' he asked.

'We're like the Clampetts – we bring one of us across the coast each year!' I said.

'Are there anymore of you likely to appear?'

'Nope, just the three of us, like the musketeers!'

Shortly after, Ben came to see Anthony and talked to him about his work with the kids in the care homes. The children he worked with were really difficult. And I mean difficult in the sense that they would throw furniture at you. Or fire a water hose down a set of stairs so people slip and fall. Or bite you. Or attack you with a knife. Genuinely, these were the most challenging kids you can imagine.

In their meeting, Ben explained to Anthony that exclusions often don't work for children with attachment disorder because they only serve to reinforce the belief that grown-ups will ignore or neglect them. They already perceive adults to be a threat, as someone who might abuse or threaten them. Given this, why would any school leader think that sending a kid home for five days, and then bringing them back would change their behaviour? Not only will it not change anything, it can make things worse, because they take the message that they have been given up on.

The more I've thought about exclusions down the years, the more they infuriate me. Writing people off is terrible. How can you ever get to the point where you write a child off?

Lots of school leaders don't take this view, I know. Time and again I see schools where the results have shot up and it is largely because they immediately excluded loads of kids, often permanently. Exclusions rates have rocketed up across the country over the past few years. The argument from heads who exclude liberally is that badly-behaving pupils are putting the education of their fellow students at risk. I understand that. Every child deserves to have an education and no one should be routinely disturbed.

Most kids will respond to some intervention, though. The trick is finding the right route. I truly believe that both staff and pupils can be kept in education if you look for bespoke approaches. I don't say this as someone who is naïve. I've met some kids who really take the biscuit. In the last few years one in particular was off-the-scale. Super-aggressive and violent, he had mental health issues and was dangerous. There was no way he could continue in a mainstream school like ours in the state that he was in. By the end, he practically lived by my side – which wasn't good for him and certainly wasn't sustainable.

We didn't exclude him, though. Lots of school leaders would have done. They'd have gone down the lengthy, legalistic procedure of putting together a file on his behaviour and then forcing him to leave and go the local pupil referral unit for excluded children. We didn't do that. To do so would have required a huge investment of our time, simply to make this lad a statistic lost to the system. A lot of children who end up in a pupil referral unit don't go on and get GCSEs. They can be labelled forever as someone who was excluded – kicking off a cycle of not going to college, not getting a job, falling into a gang or criminal activity and, eventually, getting arrested. As we all know, once young people are sent to prison, their likelihood of re-offending shoots up. By excluding, we would have created ourselves a kid who was likely to bounce in and out of institutions for the rest of his life. Instead, by giving him even half a chance, we hope he might make something of himself.

So, we set about finding somewhere suitable for him. Yes, that took phone calls, and effort, and visits. One of our staff had to go with him in a taxi to a town about 20 miles away where we found a private school able to take him in and give him the intensive care that he needs. It has cost a fortune, at a time when our school budget is already tight, but if we didn't do it, if we had just washed our hands of him, what message would that send to the community?

Back at the care home, my brother Ben took an alternative, therapeutic approach to the children he was working with. The residential was often a last-stop: kicking them out was not even an option. Hence he had been trained in de-escalation, and talking interventions. He knew techniques for getting kids to reframe their behaviour. He's also a big, friendly, character. He can make kids feel safe. In many ways, the approach he takes with the children is not so different to the one we had to deploy with our staff when first turning Harrop around: creating opportunities to talk, reframing their beliefs, and making it feel safe so that no one felt an urge to test the people around them.

Ben's skills were perfect for the school and after Ben left the school that day, Anthony sought me out. 'I want to employ him,' he said.

I was really glad. I knew it was going to make a huge difference.

'Everyone can shine, given the right lighting' – Susan Cain, The Power of Introverts

Since 2007 we've been able to create a more inclusive school and, since I took over as head, we <u>have committed to the no-exclusions policy</u>. It doesn't mean we've kept every pupil. Sometimes, as described, we've had to find somewhere else for a child to go, but the numbers are low and we have taken responsibility for that move every time. We have never pushed anyone out.

When I say we don't exclude, I also mean we don't exclude for the things that elsewhere will automatically get children thrown out. Lots of schools have automatic kick-out policies for weapons or drugs. We don't need to have that policy because our kids don't bring weapons to schools. If they did, we'd deal with it. But so far it hasn't come up – probably because the kids know they will get caught, and they know there will be repercussions that they won't like even if it isn't an exclusion.

I have less time for people who insist on zero-tolerance policies when it comes to drugs. Let me give you an example. Recently I heard about some pupils who were excluded because their school had a drugs-related policy. Fair enough, that's their choice. But the exclusion meant they would face disproportionate repercussions and these were not inherently bad lads. They had made foolish mistakes. Putting them into the pupil referral unit, half-way through their studies, would make it very unlikely they would get their GCSEs. They would also have likely been eaten alive by the other kids in the unit who were excluded over more serious behaviours. That's a quick way to derail their prospects of a productive adult life.

So instead of leaving them to the local pupil referral unit, I had an agreement with the executive head there that we could yo-yo the kids out of the unit – so they never even really started – and into our Harrop Fold. By making sure their feet didn't touch the ground in the unit we had a better chance of showing them that they weren't being given up on, that we believed they deserved a second chance, and that we cared about what happened to them. Someone had to take responsibility for them and we had the resources to do so because we've chosen to invest in them. Since then they've done really well and got through to the end of their studies.

'Do what is right, not what is easy'

I expect that we will get some stick over our exclusions policy as part of the *Educating Greater Manchester* attention. People will question if having so many kids with challenges means we are taking away from the education of other children who want to get on and learn. It is an issue

I struggle with and I'm going be totally honest: sometimes, the children who are doing well get less of our attention. Sometimes, resources are diverted. Paying to privately educate the child who I mentioned before with mental health issues means that we have less money to spend on something else.

But my view is that we, as school leaders, have to manage that. The kids also have to learn to manage that. Out in the world, as a society, we can't just wash our hands of problems. Prisons cost money. Every pound not spent now on a child's education will cost further down the line.

Plus, when our kids grow up they are going to have to learn to deal with idiotic behaviour. It happens everywhere. In the workplace, on a night out. People behave inappropriately all over the place. We have to help them deal with that by getting them to manage their own behaviour, which includes not being distracted by others who are reluctant to knuckle down at work. And also realising that the needs of others might be more important than yours at the present time.

It's often easy to jump to simplistic rules about behaviour, believing that these are important for managing children without realising that those same rules stop the kids from learning valuable lessons. Banning mobile phones in schools is the perfect example. It's a stupid idea. What person is not going to use a mobile phone in their working and personal life? Banning mobiles is running away from the issue.

Loads of our kids have their timetable on their phone. At the end of break they get their phone, they take a look, they see where they are going next. This is not a strange thing to do. My diary is on my phone; same as it is for loads of adults. It's better than a piece of paper that crumbles up and can get lost. And how about being able to take a photograph of the whiteboard and send it to yourself for revision? Or a picture of your work, together with a message from your teacher, to let them know how well you're doing? These are things I encourage kids to do.

There is no use in washing our hands of smartphones. It is our job to teach kids how to use them productively. That way, when they get to the workplace they won't suddenly think to themselves, 'oh great, I've got my phone so I'll start chatting on WhatsApp.' Instead we show them how they should use their phone and how to turn it off when you have to listen or concentrate on your work.

One of the saddest things about schools that don't allow phones is they are missing out on loads of technology that help kids learn better. Why shouldn't the pupils use Google Translate in language lessons? They will when they go on holiday. Why wouldn't you use a phone to run quick quizzes and check how many kids understand a concept? Here's why: too many heads don't want the hassle. They want to avoid the pain of having to say, 'we don't use our phones for this, we use it for that' and then following up with reinforcements or sanctions.

They also say that some children simply can't be trusted. And they are right. There will always be a kid that takes things too far. One who will push the boundaries, just like I might have done as a child! There's always at least one kid testing to see how much they can get away with in any situation. My mum didn't ban blancmange from the dinner table, though.

Likewise, my brother Ross has a habit of taking pens apart. Empty pen barrels have been used as spitball shooters by kids for decades. We don't ban pens! We deal with the misbehaviour and let everyone else carry on with their biros.

Going for a hardline 'none of this' and 'none of that' approach is simply not preparation for real life. This isn't the 1950s. We're not just out of a war with a need to raise compliant kids in case there's a fresh round of conscription. Life is complicated and kids need to be prepared for all the challenges it brings. They need the resilience, flexibility and responsibility to live modern life. Banning things is not the best way to teach that.

'I invest in people. I think people first; projects second' – Bruno Zhange We

So what do we do at Harrop Fold that's different in terms of managing behaviour compared to what is happening in other schools? Largely

restorahve
justice.

it's about the diversity of people we employ to manage the kids' needs. Most schools have an inclusion unit of some kind, where the pupils who are causing problems in classrooms will be placed. We have something similar to that but we've adapted it over the years so it has moved from being a place where kids are dumped as a punishment to something much more sophisticated.

Ben made a huge difference. At first, we had him working in the unit, with the kids who couldn't cope with being in a classroom, which is what most schools still do. But, applying the theory that a short spell in another room is unlikely to change their behaviour, we used Ben's training to start delivering therapeutic interventions. Things like anger management courses, reframing techniques, ways of keeping them calm under pressure.

We also investigated restorative justice as this was something Ben felt was helpful in the work he had done previously. Our children are startlingly honest. They are able to communicate what happened and why. The thing they don't always understand is the impact they are having on the world beyond themselves. Restorative justice is a way of having them see, sometimes visually, sometimes by listening, the consequences of their misbehaviour, and then giving sanctions which help resolve the issue and also support re-entry. Some kids experience a great deal of shame when they have done something wrong and the extent of that is so overwhelming they can't easily go back into the classroom. Working restoratively helps them overcome this step and can get them back on track.

At Harrop the system has now moved on again. Ben's main work is now outside of the unit, patrolling the corridors, and proactively looking for issues. If kids are kicking off in a classroom a member of staff can radio through to Ben and he will turn up within a few minutes. He can then start the process of calming and reintegrating the child before he or she is removed and placed in the inclusion unit. This avoids having kids bounce in and out of classrooms on temporary exclusions and addresses behaviour problems at their source.

An on-call system is not unique to us. Lots of schools have something similar. What matters is that the person who turns up to the classroom actually makes a sustainable difference. If a school leader simply comes along, shouts at kids, gets them quiet, and then walks out again without any expectation they will return, the likelihood is that the lesson will go downhill. Think back to our Ross's first lesson. The assistant head brought the year 9 pupils up, quiet as mice. He walked away saying 'good luck' *knowing* they would kick off. Why do that? A smarter leader would have reminded the pupils of expectations and, as they stepped away, reminded them that if there were any issues that he would be back and deal with them. Teachers should not feel like they are on their own dealing with the impossible.

Another potentially unique aspect of what we do is that we have graded call-outs which get different types of responses. You might have a senior member like me turn up if a whole class is causing a problem. Or, if it's an individual child, Ben is very skilled in knowing whether or not he can put a child back into a lesson or whether he needs to withdraw them and work with them individually. Another staff member, Lauren, has developed our Bridge Unit, which works with children in the exclusion unit who we are trying to get back into lessons but have emotion-related needs, for example anxiety or depression.

Having this flexibility in approaches is important. Humans are complex beings so we've got to have different approaches for different problems. It's not just about having a process, either. It's about having the right people with the right strengths. It was building up a comprehensive skillset across our staff that helped us move to the no-exclusions mindset.

One thing I also want to make clear is that I'm not into the idea that some kids respond better to a man or a woman when it comes to behaviour. I don't think that's true at all. It's about the character of the person who turns up and the needs of the individual. Sometimes I've seen kids respond well to Ben precisely because he is big and can be intimidating in the way he holds his size. This shows kids that get worked up about intimidating someone that there will always be bigger, tougher, harder guys in the world. But not every kid needs that.

Really, it's like how any good team operates. In rugby you need players in different positions who are good at different things. Everyone has to handle the basics: running, tackling, taking knocks. A player can be called on to do these things at any time. Great teams know who is the best at each thing and plan their strategy accordingly. You put people in the positions where their strengths will make the biggest difference.

Schools are no different. As Jim Collins, who wrote the famous business book *Good to Great* once said, great leaders worry about the 'who' before anything else.

He said, 'They start by getting the right people on the bus, the wrong people off the bus, and the right people in the right seats.'

This flips a lot of thinking on its head. Many people think that school leaders should start with the strategy – 'where' it is they want to take the school – and then back-fill the positions you need to get there. Collins' extensive research of top businesses which beat the performance odds over a long period of time shows this isn't the right approach. Successful leaders put people first, every time. They select people who they know will work hard, put them in positions that use their strengths, and enable them to get on with it.

***

Getting the school to a point where there are no exclusions, when previously there had been hundreds, was an amazing example of how an organisation can change if you re-imagine what is possible.

By 2009, however, I had to re-imagine what was possible for myself too. Anthony announced that he was going to step down after six years at the helm. Harrop Fold was suddenly on the hunt for a new headteacher.

Chapter 8 –
The unexpected headteacher

'A boss says go, a leader says 'let's go" – EM Kelly

When Anthony announced he was moving on as head my first thought was that it wasn't a surprise. Throughout six years in the role he had given absolutely everything he could, getting the school out of special measures and on the way to becoming the place it is today. From the start he was an 'executive head' – more a strategic role than an operational one – and this was his second successful turnaround, after the one he achieved at Falmer High School in Brighton. He was getting regular job offers and it was right for him to have another challenge. (He's now Chief Executive of the Landau Forte Charitable Trust, running six schools across the Midlands.)

Right up to the moment he said he was leaving, I never thought I would become a headteacher. It's not a title I find easy to identify with, even now. I love the school, and I love leading it, but if I wasn't doing this job at Harrop Fold specifically, I don't think I'd want to do it elsewhere.

However, once he was going, I knew it was the job I most wanted. I was already an operational head as Anthony was often out doing executive level roles across other schools. Hence, I was straight with the governors. I told them that I wasn't always a person who did things in an orthodox way but I really wanted to be a champion for the kids and the community. I wanted to lead Harrop Fold. It was brilliant that they trusted me enough to take it on and offered me the job.

A lot of people think headship is about hiding away in an office, but I've always been more hands-on. I remember, soon after I became a headteacher, that a National Leader of Education – a school leader who helps others – came to the school to see me. We were chatting in my office when a call came through saying two intruders were stalking around the playground. I asked the lady if she wanted to come with me while I dealt with it or if she would prefer to stay in the office. She shuffled nervously out into the corridor with me and followed me outside.

As we were walking across the playground she kept saying, 'you shouldn't be doing this, you shouldn't be doing this.' I was baffled. I told her not to worry. 'We'll just find out who they are and what they are doing.' I'd manned the doors at nightclubs in Warrington! I wasn't too worried about a couple of lads walking around on a field in the middle of the day.

Across the yard I noticed a couple of ordinary-looking lads in their early 20s. Jackets, caps, nothing unusual. I went over and asked what they were doing. 'We're on our way to see [some name I don't remember]', one of them replied.

'Well, you can't come through here,' I told them. 'You'll have to go back out and walk around the school.'

'Why?' they asked.

'Because it's a school, lads. It's a safe environment. We can't have you walking around when we don't know who you are. Even the teachers have to sign in,' I explained.

'Oh right, yeah, sound,' the lads said, and, with minimal fuss, I walked them off the site.

That was the end of the matter as far as I was concerned. The National Leader was mortified and gave me a lecture on how escorting people off-site should be someone else's job.

I found this the weirdest conversation. In all my time at Harrop Fold I've never had anyone push me. But, more than that, why should a headteacher let someone else be pushed instead of going and dealing with the situation themselves? That's terrible leadership. If I'm expecting anyone else to escort people off the premises, then I should be willing to do it myself too.

Unfortunately this was not the only time I would find myself at odds with the values of other school leaders, especially Ofsted inspectors. I know some people view my way of running things as a bit 'quirky'. But it's all done for a purpose.

Culture at Harrop is important to all of us. People come to the school and talk about the positive vibe. In fact, we're such a strong community we refer to ourselves as 'Team Harrop'. It shows we work together towards our goals.

Anthony instilled the mentality that change was possible at Harrop but I wanted to take our teamwork to the next level. I had to wait at first. Anthony was well-respected, so I couldn't just rush in with a new plan. I had to give people time to adjust.

I've long had an interest in leadership theories so I started paying more and more attention to what was happening in the most successful organisations across the world – in sport, art, technology, everywhere – and began constructing ideas of how to make that work now that I was in charge.

'Re-imagine, don't rebuild'

As I touched on a little earlier, one word that has really struck a chord with me is 're-imagine'. It is the title of a book by the American business writer, Tom Peters, and he, in turn, was inspired by a group of New York architects who took out an advert after 9/11 carrying the message 'Don't rebuild, re-imagine'. I love Tom Peters' work and continue to follow him to this day. *See P.8*

That is what my brother Ross had to do to become a better teacher, and it was also the mindset our school needed to get out of special measures. Now, though, I was asking myself: 'how can I push the concept even further?'

I wanted to put people first. As you already know, I had also been inspired by another American business writer, Jim Collins, who argues that assembling the right team should be your greatest priority in building any organisation. Having listened to so much leadership theory, I created my 3P Model – 'People, Process and Performance'. Put 'people' first, get them to generate the 'process' for how things will work, and then the 'performance' will happen.

More than that, though, I wanted everyone employed at Harrop Fold to re-imagine how the school would work. I can already hear you asking: 'but what does that actually mean'? Well, re-imagining has five steps: creating, innovating, trying, failing and having fun along the way.

You can only be creative if the circumstances and context are right. I knew that, as a leader, I needed to create a safe environment where people could share their ideas out loud, and especially when they had a suggestion that was brand new or even outlandish. It is no use asking people for thoughts on how to improve a school if they only say things that have already been tried.

The 'innovation' stage is about acting on this creativity and coming up with concrete methods for how to implement these new ideas. You then try out the innovation – 'try' being the third stage of re-imagining.

It's so important to have a go at things – to actually put new ideas to the test. If you look at models like Kaizen, a Japanese improvement system used by Toyota, they rely on an iterative process. People make suggestions, try them out and see which ones make incremental improvements. With our team, so long as it wasn't a huge risk, I wanted them to try new things. To this day, I still want to see that. Sitting still is not going to get us the performance we need.

The fourth stage of re-imagining is failure. If we are truly being creative, then it is inevitable that some of the things we try will not succeed. If we learn from those experiences, that's okay. Again, it's an iterative process. In *Black Box Thinking* by Matthew Syed, he talks about the benefits of learning from failure.

Finally, re-imagining should always be fun as long as it is done in an optimistic atmosphere. I am a realistic optimist. I tell people when I interview them that Harrop will be one of the most exhausting places they will ever work, but also one of the most exhilarating. They will always be encouraged to bring their ideas to the table, and have them tried out and improved upon over time. They will have the chance to re-imagine what we do, and to make it happen.

Silly little things have made a difference to how people feel about work. Before meetings we might get everyone to tell a joke, or describe a fact about themselves people would be surprised to know. This helps to relax the tension and gets people feeling more creative.

To give space for re-imagining, we also use several tools for gathering ideas. We have breakfasts on a Friday every two or three weeks where all staff can come – cleaners, everyone. Senior leaders serve coffee and we put on a buffet breakfast. I make protein porridge, which some people turn their nose up at, but it's popular, honestly! It's a great opportunity for staff to relax, catch up and talk to colleagues with whom they might not normally connect. We might share positive stories from the week or discuss new ideas.

'Don't talk about the X factor, talk about the WHY factor'

Putting people first doesn't mean just letting everyone do what they want. Organisations need an underlying purpose, which every member of the team is striving to attain. In sport, the team wants to win. At Harrop Fold, I knew when I took over that the staff would need to help me uncover what our purpose should be.

Again, I know this approach is unusual. Lots of headteachers come in with a ready-made vision for the school and set about getting everyone in line as quickly as possible. Leaders who operate like this get a lot of praise. People in education often talk about an 'X factor' when they see a super-head come in and change everything overnight. But I find this need for speed a major concern. Decades of management writing make plain that there is rarely a quick fix. Change brought about by force of charisma is often short-termist and shallow.

It is worth learning the lesson of Herb Kelleher, CEO of Southwest Airlines, an incredibly successful low-cost carrier the US. He developed his organisation in such a way that if he had to be called away, any other person could run the company in his place. That was possible because everyone understood, and bought into, the core purpose that underpinned all decision-making.

At Harrop we needed long term, positive, sustainable change which wasn't just being driven by me. I wanted people to shift away from thinking I was going to bring an 'X factor' and instead get them thinking about the purpose or 'WHY factor' for our school. Why we were all getting up in a morning and getting ourselves into school? What were we striving for?

So, one very cold, wet January – straight after the Christmas holiday – we devoted an entire staff training day to the question: 'Why do you choose to work at Harrop Fold?'

I stood up in front of the bleary-eyed teachers, still fragile from their frantic holidays, and pushed them for answers.

'Why are you here?' I asked. 'Here, we have the biggest class sizes. In other schools you could be teaching classes of 20 kids. This is a challenging community. We don't exclude anyone. You will have to deal with behaviour issues that other schools never even see once. So why work here when you could earn more money and have less hassle somewhere else? Why do you work at Harrop?'

There were moans and groans to start (it was the first day) but it sparked the most amazing dialogue.

Everyone has their own unique story about why they came to Harrop Fold. We have two ex-professional rugby players who came to learn about teaching then fell in love with the place and stayed. A number of former students came back to work at the school because they believe in what we do. One former pupil, who was here when it was in special measures, is now a head of department.

In the end, taking all these different paths and ideas, we whittled all the stories for why people worked at Harrop Fold down to three things:

- adding value

- helping young people aspire to more

- making a long-term difference

If you work in a school where most parents are educated and you teach classes of 20 children, none of whom have behavioural problems, you can certainly add some value. But at Harrop the value is so much more. We take children who can't read and make sure they do so by the time they leave. We can be the difference between a kid getting good enough grades to get into college and them not getting any grades at all. We can help a child see that they have more options in life than to join the family business or get caught up in crime. We learned that those challenges are precisely why our staff get up in the morning and come and work in some of the most challenging circumstances facing any school in England.

Two weeks later, during a staff gathering, we put out a SurveyMonkey vote asking all staff to decide which of these three things – adding value, helping aspiration and making a difference – would become our ultimate purpose. Our ultimate 'WHY' factor.

'Making a difference' received 92% of the votes. We had our purpose at last. Or so I thought.

Two weeks later, during another staff briefing, I wanted to end by re-iterating our new WHY. 'Don't forget,' I said, 'we are here to make a difference.'

One of the front office staff put up her hand. 'We don't think it's about making a difference,' she said, 'what we do here is make *the* difference.'

The room started nodding. I had been pulled up short. They were absolutely right. Schools make a difference, and that's important, but at Harrop Fold, because of the position we're in and the community we serve, we make the difference.

Creating a shared purpose with our staff, rather than handing them something I had already formulated in my head, was vital to creating our 'Team Harrop' ethos. Making the difference is our agreed principle. It drives everything. Like Herb Kelleher at Southwest Airlines, I know

that if I am ever called away, every other member of staff will make decisions based on this principle. Which is much better than handing everyone a pre-made vision that they may not support when the boss's back is turned.

***

Before creating our overall purpose, the staff believed in Harrop and wanted to be part of it. But what we didn't have was a shared language for talking about what it meant to us. The shared purpose meant we could now explain and discuss what we meant, and put it at the centre of our decision-making.

Here's a concrete example of that. We use our purpose – making *the* difference – in the way we recruit new members of staff.

When we are looking for new staff members we want them to have three things: character, competence and chemistry, in that order. When recruiting, we always ask, 'Will you be a person that makes *the* difference, not a difference?' We explain that our WHY is very important. We describe honestly where the school is at and about how behaviour works and our challenges. Some people say, 'This is a fantastic way of working, but it's not for me.' Other people say, 'This is absolutely where I want to work!' In that case, we know if they are the right sort of character for the school and we can move forward to look at competence and chemistry. If our central purpose doesn't fire them up, then there's no point. Remember: you've got to start by getting the right people on the bus, and the wrong ones off. There's no point battling against people who want something different to what the rest of the team wants. People first, always.

'We have a strategic plan, it's called doing things' – Herb Kelleher, former CEO of Southwest Airlines

So far, you know that at Harrop Fold:

Our WHY: is making the difference.

Our HOW: is through the people in our team.

Figuring out WHAT to do to make the difference to our pupils was the third part of the puzzle.

Activity is not the same as achievement, so figuring out how we should prioritise our time was, and still is, a constant source of healthy debate.

Every two weeks we vote, as a school, on what our focus should be over the coming fortnight – either at our team briefings, or online through SurveyMonkey. If someone isn't confident enough to speak up at briefings I encourage people to bring ideas to their line manager, who can then raise them with me.

The fortnightly focus is something everyone should know and be able to discuss: from the front of school staff through to senior managers. It's about everyone at Team Harrop being on the same page.

This is also when we might try something new.

A recent example is how we focused on quick starts to learning. The beginning of a school lesson involves meeting pupils, getting them into seats and getting them learning. We wanted staff to focus on getting this crucial part of each lesson down to three minutes or less.

Staff got creative. Some used timers. Others gave tests at the beginning of lessons. One faculty focused on detentions for lateness; they wanted to see if a negative approach was better than a positive one. We focused on the topic for three weeks like we always do. Why three weeks? That's how long it takes to form a habit.

As we went along we shared which things worked and each set of teachers came up with a set of techniques that worked for their department.

For another three weeks we focused on tracking progress and discovered a system based on video controls – fast forward, pause, and stop – worked really well. In lessons, staff would use the language of those four phrases to reflect on progress with pupils. We now have indicators up in classrooms which can be used for this purpose.

At the end of the three weeks we have an honest conversation based on two questions. First, did we (the staff) do what we said we would do? Sometimes the activities we planned are not done properly. Various reasons cause this. Maybe staff were distracted by another event and teachers didn't actually focus on starting the learning in the lesson properly but instead focused on behaviour? When we realise that we haven't stuck to our plan we consider running the initiative again and addressing the reasons why it did not work the first time.

Second, did the task do what we wanted? Did the kids actually start learning quicker, or track progress better? This tells us if the activities worked and whether we should roll out changes across the school, or if we should cut our losses. After all, not every whole-school focus works: some tank in spectacular fashion.

Probably the worst focused intervention we made was trying to get kids to drink healthily. It opened the biggest can of worms. I passionately believe in healthy drinking and eating. Having children limit their intake of sugary drinks is obviously a good thing. Our intention was absolutely pure and the staff were totally on-side.

What we didn't realise was that a school policy of healthy drinking is almost impossible to police. At first, we thought the simplest way to make children healthy was to say they could only drink water. The problem? They simply didn't drink it. To paraphrase an old adage: you can drag a Harrop Fold pupil to water, but you can't make him or her drink! We then said 'only healthy drinks'. But what's a healthy drink? Is Coke Zero a healthy drink because it's sugar free? Is a fruit juice drink healthy when it's packed with sugar? We could have banned fizzy drinks but the canteen sold them and couldn't just stop.

After weeks of agonising over the whole thing, we asked the most critical question: was this issue fundamentally affecting learning? The answer was no. We had no evidence our hours of fussing over fluids was making any difference except distracting us from our core purpose. So we stopped it.

Do I still wish every kid at Harrop Fold was drinking and eating the best possible nutrients? Definitely. But we had to accept that it wasn't where we should be putting our biggest efforts.

Acrylic fingernails are another issue we considered pursuing as a whole-school focus and then decided against. A member of staff had raised the issue of pupils coming into school with brightly-coloured impractical fake nails. We thought about having a clamp-down for our three-week focus. But, how many students does the issue actually affect? When we thought about it carefully, only around 20 out of the 800 pupils were wearing the nails. Our psychological bias towards negative issues meant we almost put everyone's efforts into changing a behaviour that was affecting about 3% of the cohort rather than looking at a teaching issue affecting every pupil. That's ridiculous. Far better to deal with the false-nailed pupils on an individual basis, and run a genuine whole-school focus for our intervention.

As a leader, the job is often about clearing the wood from the trees. In our case that means separating the niggly issues – things like nails and soft drinks – from those that are actually making the difference to learning.

***

Did this focus on people and process work? Thankfully, it did.

In 2010, nine months after I took over the job, the school finally achieved a 'good' rating.

Three years later, we did it again. This time, the lead inspector came in to see me and said, verbatim: 'We are not quite sure what this "Team Harrop" thing is Drew, but we do know that it is working for you.'

The words 'Team Harrop' appear three times in the two-page Ofsted summary. We are proud of that. Team Harrop is about a whole group of people – me, Ross, Ben and thousands of others – coming together around a culture of wanting to make the biggest and best difference that we can. As I've said before, Ofsted grades are not what matters to me. That the inspectors recognised the power of our team meant absolutely everything.

In 2013 we also achieved our highest results, when 57% of pupils achieved at least five passes in their GCSEs including English and Maths. That was above the national average for all schools that year – something which is particularly impressive given so many of our pupils are behind in their learning when they first arrive at Harrop Fold.

We were lauded for those results. I was invited to speak to the Department for Education, and at leadership conferences, and to give the story of our turnaround success. It was great to be asked, and I hope people were able to learn about the great things we were doing. But I would also advise caution.

One of the things people outside of education often fail to understand is that there are massive cohort effects. Each year, you get given a group of pupils who are a diverse mix of kids, and you have no control over their personal foibles. It's a bit like when you have children. They come with ready-made personalities and interests. You can mould their behaviour but they still each have their own quirks (just like us Povey brothers!).

Some year groups gel together easily and, for reasons that are more to do with luck than hard work, work brilliantly well. In 2013, we had a good year group and, in some cases, we got lucky. A large number of children on the borderline of getting a pass grade snuck in by a point or so. In other years, however, we've had a number of children just miss out. And in those years our results look worse.

Grades are clearly important. Every year I am devastated that we are not getting a higher number of passes for all our kids. It makes such a difference to their future and it's what we aim for. But I am also realistic about the influence we have at school. Sometimes, for no good reason, a year group doesn't gel together and things don't work as well. Sometimes the pupils don't just sneak over the line. It's great to be complimented on those years when our results go up, but we have to keep perspective even when they go down. What we are doing at Harrop Fold is building sustainable, gradual improvements so that our average gets better over time.

***

If all this makes headship sound like a doddle then it's because I've chosen to focus on the positive, rather than the massive hole in the road that appeared when I took over the role.

The truth is, shortly before I became the headteacher I found out that the school had a £3 million debt, and every penny needed to be paid back. We would get no extra cash to cover it. In fact, school budgets have fallen in real-terms over the past decade by around 5%. For every £1 going into schools in 2010 we are now getting the equivalent of 95p. Yet, out of that, we were expected to pay back £3 million – and if I didn't, the debt would keep mounting and, in all likelihood, the school would need to close.

Five years of hard work – and suddenly, our success was as fragile as ever.

Chapter 9 –
An unexpected bump

'Anyone can give up. It's the easiest thing in the world to do. But holding it together when everyone in the world expects you to fall apart? That's true strength' – Chris Bradford

So, how did it happen? That's the first question most people ask when learning Harrop Fold had a £3 million deficit in 2010. 'Who let it get that far out of hand?'

The truth is that no one person is culpable. When the school was deigned 'the worst in the country' it was in the interests of politicians to deliver a quick fix. The Department for Education, overseen through the 2000s by a series of Labour ministers, was happy to throw money at the problem. The council likewise. Anthony, who was the headteacher, was encouraged to get consultants in, and hire good people.

Operating the school on two sites before 2008 was expensive and no money had been given for the cost of shuttling staff on buses between the two plus the necessary additional staff needed to run a split-site school. When the £24 million new building was signed off by the Treasury, there was no thought for how it would be paid back.

'Just spend the money,' we were told, 'you'll never have to pay it back.'

These actions would come back to haunt us. Not the people who actually made the decisions, of course: they were long gone. But they have haunted Harrop Fold for the past seven years.

Most of the cash given to schools from central government is based on how many pupils you teach. Each child is assigned a lump sum of around £5,000 (depending on where you are in the country plus a few other variables).

New buildings like ours, built under the Private Finance Initiative (PFI) scheme, have a rental cost, which we pay back each year. Theoretically, that is also based on the number of pupils. For example, you might be required to pay £500 per year per child.

This all sounds fair and reasonable. But the devil is in the detail. If the number of pupils attending your school should fall, then you will indeed get less cash from the government – and yet the PFI rental rate does not actually change. That is because the per-child rent is always based on estimated pupil numbers from the date when the school opened. Even if you suddenly have half the number of students, and therefore half the cash, the school still must pay a whacking great annual fee.

By 2010, our pupil numbers had fallen from an estimated 1,200 to 600. This is not unusual in a school which has been in special measures or rated only as 'satisfactory' for several years. Mud sticks. It's like Skoda. When it was taken over in the 1990s, its reputation for reliability dropped through the floor. It took the best part of a decade for them to turn things around. Even today some people still laugh at the name. Likewise, only after we started getting 'good' ratings did our numbers go up.

Salford council's failure to close another nearby school also didn't help. When our building was originally designed, the planners drew it up for 1,200 pupils because St George's, a local Roman Catholic school, was supposed to be closing. That plan was overturned by an independent adjudicator, and consequently we only had half our places filled.

I also need to be honest about wages. At one point, they were out of control. In the early days of Harrop Fold going into special measures, consultants had been parachuted in to turn things around. Some were on almost £90,000 a year – a lot now, but even more back then. One of the first senior meetings I went to had 14 people in it.

For several years, then – and in some part for good reason – the school had spent more than it had coming in. It was now in serious trouble.

That said, I do strongly believe that if the financial crash had not happened, this debt wouldn't have mattered. Throughout the 2000s education was awash with money and we were constantly told it would be paid off. If you look at some of the bail-outs given to failing academies in recent years, you can see money is still available where it suits the government's pet projects.

For example, nearly £10 million was spent on a vocational school in Daventry, in the Midlands, which was such a failure it closed after a few years and the cash was written off. Bolton Wanderers Free School, just a stone's throw away from here, lasted two years before it had to close. It cost millions when it was open and closed with over half a million still outstanding in debt, which has now been wiped away.

Our problem was that we hit our peak deficit at the wrong time. As a school overseen by the local council, we were not one of the academy schools the Conservative government favoured with cash when they got into power in 2010. Instead, under the guise of austerity, they pulled the purse strings tight. Hands that were once generous in doling out the cash now started trying to grab it all back.

'We have no money. We shall have to think' – Winston Churchill

When I first found out about the debt, I didn't tell the whole staff, just the senior team. I decided to try and argue it out with the local council, who we owe the money to directly, asking them to go back to the education department and tell them it just wasn't possible to repay. 'This is between you and the government,' I would say. 'You told us to spend the money so you need to put your hands in your pockets.'

National consultants and experts were sent in to help me. Cocksure and confident, they would come in and tell me everything would be fine. Then they'd look at the books and realise a deficit this size had never been seen nationally before. They all left with the same sentiment: 'It's impossible. You can't do it.'

The worst aspect of a school deficit (particularly at this level) is the impact on pupils. The only way to pay such a sum back is to cut spending allocated for the education of the young people at our school. Since 2010 our children's entire secondary education has been limited by the deficit, which is a tragedy. The combination of wanting to secure radical school improvement alongside a reduced spend per pupil is a Gordian knot.

Once I accepted that the debt would have to be paid, I knew that I had different options for how to do it. I could stay in the office, pore over the books and decide what I was going to do. Or, I could stick to my faith in Team Harrop, and go out and speak to the staff. All of them. It was no use downloading my stress onto a few chosen senior leaders. We were all in this problem together and we were going to get out of it, together.

Committing to honest, clear and calm conversations is a lovely idea, but I was worried about spreading gloom and anxiety. Avoiding that meant finding a way to galvanise people rather than delivering the bad news as a body blow.

We gathered into a staff meeting and I stood in front of everyone and explained the situation.

'We are in £3 million of debt. I'm angry about it and I've tried to solve it, but the council and government are not budging. So I need your help. I need us, together, to figure out how we are going to pay this money off. We are going to have to tighten our belts in obvious ways, but I also need solutions from you.'

The staff were obviously shocked. It was by far the biggest debt in the country. If you asked most businesses to go from a standing start to bringing in an additional £3 million over the next few years they would struggle to do so. We couldn't even bring extra money in. We were going to have to do it purely through cutbacks – as well as by reducing our expenditure so that we were no longer adding to the debt.

The room was quiet at first. I worried that I was asking too much.

Then Chris, a woman from the front office, raised her hand.

'Second class, Mr. Povey,' Chris said. 'Second class!'

I didn't understand what she meant.

'We can use second class stamps, Mr Povey. In the office. I've just worked it out in my head and if we used second class then I think we'd save about £1,400 a year.'

That was amazing. A total breakthrough.

'Yes!' I said, 'This is the sort of thinking we need. That's £1,400. Who's got something more?'

Another hand went up. And then another, and another.

The head of maths offered up his budget for resources. We looked again at lighting, at heating, at how we were buying pens and pencils. We decided to make our class sizes bigger. We had to look at our staffing and make serious reductions. We offered voluntary severance and early retirement. People helped us out by taking up the offers. In the end, we reduced staff by 67% compared to when I started – a drastic cut.

It made the job tougher, for sure. But by the end of 2010 we had a million pounds' worth of savings.

Since then we've paid off £1.3 million of our debt. That's about £186,000 a year on average. All while covering interest payments and the rest. If we hadn't paid that money off, the debt would now be £6.7 million. Although that's still less than the £10 million the Department for Education wrote off in 12 months for failed academies and free schools.

The million pound in-year savings in 2010 got us to the point where we could actually start paying off the debt – rather than just servicing it. We are still figuring out how to clear the backlog.

Until now, we haven't made the community aware of the issue. We didn't want it to damage us locally. What school wants to be in the newspaper saying that they are underfunded every week when they are trying to build a reputation for excellence?

Today we are oversubscribed and have a strong reputation, so it's no longer as dangerous for us to talk about this issue. And I think the local community need to know what has happened. A lot of people have become famous on the back of Harrop Fold. Awards have been handed out to people at a governmental level who played a part in our initial turnaround. Yet where are those people now that we are fighting to sustain the progress, while paying off the goods they chucked at us? They've walked away and left us holding the baby.

I am also still fighting with the government and council about the debt. I will never, ever accept that it was right for us to be put in this position, and so I will never, ever stop believing that a more just solution can be found. Every week I call someone about it. The Department for Education must dread my calls! I'm not going to stop until someone does something about it, though.

One of the reasons for doing the television series, and this book, was the hope that someone like Richard Branson might come along and point out how crazy the situation is. Several companies are already helping us, and I am increasingly doing leadership talks for private businesses to earn money to pay the debt off.

I never played the lottery until I found out about the debt at Harrop Fold. I play it every Saturday, now. If I won the money I'd pay off the school's debt and carry on working. That's how much I care about this situation and how badly I want it wiped away. I can see the damage it is doing and I want it ended.

Some headteachers have been unsympathetic about our situation. Many schools have struggled financially in the last few years as school budgets have been squeezed. Costs have leapt for everyone, particularly with changes in national insurance and pension contributions for teachers, but they need to understand that we are facing a perfect storm of issues. Some heads have a falling roll, so they have less cash, but they aren't paying the sky-high rent for a PFI building like we are. Others have the high rent, but their pupil numbers are okay. Others have been caught out by being over-staffed, or having a split site, or having to pay off past leadership decisions. I've yet to find anyone else who is facing all of these issues – and with £3 million inherited debt on top!

'Even though you can't expect to defeat the absurdity of the world, you must try' – Phil Ochs

If you want a case study in the craziness of government, here's a brilliant one for you. If we closed down, our debt would be erased. All our hard work would be gone. Our community hub would be gone. But we wouldn't have to worry about the debt anymore.

Here's an even more ridiculous point: if we were to go into special measures, the debt would also be written off. That's right. If Team Harrop were to stop making the difference, and go home early each day, we could get the damaging debt wiped out.

How? Well, in the event that a school like ours goes into special measures, the government is responsible for finding a charitable trust to take it over. When they do that, the debt remains with the local council. Hence, the school gets to join the charitable trust (also known as 'academy trusts') without its financial penance looming over its head. Freedom at last!

Going into a charitable academy trust has significant advantages for a school. It is why the government spent the past seven years trying to encourage every school to join one. When several schools work together it is easier to manage finances, because you can share backroom resources. For example, you can have one team working on recruitment, rather than each school employing their own human resources people.

Schools in academy chains can also share people. We are really good at managing behaviour at Harrop Fold. I know we are one of the best in this area. What we've not been able to do over the past few years, because of the debt, is be absolutely at the forefront of curriculum and lesson planning. Our teaching is top quality, but a lot of subjects have changed in recent years, and without the money to send staff on training courses, or buy in new resources, it is inevitable that there will be other schools out there who have an edge on us when it comes to academic teaching.

Thankfully we know an academy trust who are brilliant at curriculum and want to work with us, Consilium. In fact, we want to join their trust, because we know our teachers could learn from theirs about subject teaching, and our staff could train theirs in behaviour management skills. We could get all the help our pupils need, which we can't currently get from Salford council because its budget is being heavily cut.

Right now, though, we cannot join this trust because of our debt! Even though we have offered to carry on paying it off. Even though the council has said it is happy for us to repay on our own schedule. Even though we would be better placed to raise the funds as part of an academy trust than we are on our own! Despite all these things the Department for Education will not sign off on a transfer because of our debt. All because of decisions taken a decade ago, by people no longer around to face up to them.

This strikes me as absurd. At the very least, it is a failure of politicians and officials to get into a room, face facts, and deal with the problem. At times I have asked myself whether it would be better if the school did fail, so we could get ourselves out of this mess and the kids could stop suffering. But to do that would be to give up on Harrop Fold. And as I learned all those years ago in Mrs Firth's classroom: giving up on kids is the worst thing of all.

Chapter 10 – Educating Drew: What have I learned?

In the eight years I have been headteacher at Harrop Fold I've learned every bit as much as the young people who we teach. I've also learned from pupils, staff, parents, the local community, private business leaders – a whole range of people.

So, what are my 10 most important lessons from the past decade?

Besides the quotes throughout this book, I would say there are 10 key mantras I have learned.

1. Everyone needs a safe environment

2. Keep your eyes, ears, mind and heart open, and listen four times more than you speak

3. Be patient: things take longer than you expect

4. Always be learning (and not just from other educators)

5. It's not about competing, it's about completing

6. Leadership doesn't have to be lonely

7. Stand up for the profession

8. Nothing comes without risk

9. Ofsted is just one piece of information

10. Giving hope during difficult times is the vital leadership skill

1. Everyone needs a safe environment

Abraham Maslow made this point back in the 1960s with his hierarchy of needs and it remains true today. Every human needs to know they are safe. First, all people need to know they have physical security. That no one is going to attack them and they will have somewhere safe to sleep with enough food to eat and water to drink. But security is also mental and emotional. People need to feel they can live their life without being ridiculed or insulted or left on their own.

Years ago, when Mrs Firth protected me from feeling ashamed by my stutter, she created a safe environment for me. When I was in her classroom, I didn't feel I would be laughed at for getting things wrong. Every human in the world is looking to feel as safe as I did in Mrs Firth's classroom. When they do, you get great things out of them.

One of the reasons why so many former pupils want to come back and work at Harrop Fold is because they feel safe here. They know they can flourish in the environment we build for them. How do you make people feel safe? By having an open culture where everyone is listened to and valued, and making that culture a central focus for everyone involved.

2. Keep your eyes, ears, mind and heart open, and listen four times more than you speak

Spending the first years at Harrop Fold walking around and managing problems was an eye-opener. At the start it really felt as if the value in wandering around would be the help I could give by going into lessons and talking to children. It never occurred to me the value would be in how much people wanted to be seen and heard. Yes, it mattered that I was able to take a disruptive child out of a lesson, but the most important thing for the teacher was that someone else was there to support them in dealing with the child. Turning up at the door meant the teacher no longer felt alone. The feeling of togetherness that breeds is often enough to give the member of staff the boost they need to deal with a pupil's behaviour on their own.

Likewise, when pupils do daft things in the corridor, I don't bawl them out immediately. I ask them why they are doing something. I take the time to understand. For example, if I hear a kid swearing in a corridor I want to know what has led to them betraying the school's values. They all know they shouldn't be swearing, so what is going on?

Visitors are often amazed at how honest our children are when they hear me asking these questions. It's not the honesty of children that is unusual, though. It's that too many school leaders forget to ask young people questions about their behaviour or they don't bother to listen to the answers.

For every four minutes someone else speaks, a leader should only speak for one. The staff and pupil have the information. Your job is to take it in and use it strategically, not spout out more.

3. Be patient: things take longer than you expect

Learning that change, and the implementation of policies, can take longer than you expect (or want) has been difficult for me.

When I took over the school in 2009 I wanted the exam results to rocket. In 2013 we hit our highest ever GCSE pass rate – 57%. I was chuffed to pieces, and the government were delighted too! They invited me to speak at conferences and everyone wanted to know how we did it. Then the performance league tables were changed. The government decided to remove vocational qualifications. Our kids who studied subjects like sports science were suddenly taken out of the equation. Ever since then, our results have looked less good.

My immediate reaction to seeing our result rates dropping was to double-down. I made it a central focus and we've run ourselves ragged trying to improve them. Teachers have run revision classes in holidays. They have gone to kids' houses to get them in for exams. The staff come in at weekends, holidays, everything. And yet it hasn't shifted the needle as much as I've wanted and I've found it devastating.

Real change takes time. We were good at the vocational qualifications and shifting over to the new system requires a transition that staff need to prepare for and train in. It's like expecting a competitive sprinter to do 100 metre dashes one month and then win at marathons the next month. It can't be done. Hence, I've had to learn that our improvements may be slow and gradual.

As a team we are also thinking about whether we ought to be chasing results in the subjects the government says it prefers our pupils to take. For example, because of the way the government has designed the league tables, schools are under pressure to make sure every child is entered for a GCSE in modern foreign languages. Are we really better off putting a child in for a French exam in which we know they will get a D grade rather than putting them in for a sports coaching qualification which they could pass with flying colours? The D grade is better for our league tables, but the coaching qualification may be better for a job. It's tough for school leaders to ignore government wants, but I'm starting to wonder if it might be the right thing.

Instead of focusing on exam results, it may be better to think about other indicators that matter to our pupils. School attendance, for example, has improved enormously. Attending school is highly correlated with better exam results. Hence, if we make sure our kids turn up, then going forward we will be establishing a good baseline for better results – whether in the exams the government wants, or any other type of qualification. This might be an avenue for us to explore.

I've also had to re-evaluate the idea that 'more' focus is always 'better'. I'm a driven person, and always want to eke the last bit of improvement out of the Harrop team. Sometimes, however, you can push so far that performance is harmed.

An example of this is getting teachers and pupils so focused on revision before the exam season that it actually freaks out the young people. Last year I read an article about John Tomsett, a headteacher in York, who pulled back from having extra revision sessions for his pupils. John noticed that all the extra revision sessions were tiring out the staff and the pupils right when they most needed to relax. Relying on the extra classes also meant teachers weren't always putting in as much thought to embedding learning throughout the year. Teachers started feeling that every child would catch up during the extra revision sessions. A more sustainable approach, of course, is to ensure knowledge is taught in memorable ways the first time around – and not loading everyone up with extra work at exam time!

Ultimately, I have had to learn that I can't simply expect or demand change to happen quickly. Impatience is not an improvement solution.

4. Always be learning (and not just from other educators)

A lot of headteachers did well at school, went straight to university, and then went straight back into school. School is their comfort zone. It is the place they know well: they know the intricacies of education policy and all the latest research into the craft of teaching. This is great and I love learning from those people. But school leaders can also learn from lots and lots of other places, too.

Private businesses are not always beloved in the education sector but people like Richard Branson, Tom Peters and Jim Collins in the business world have done amazing things which school leaders can, and should, learn from. The literature on positive psychology – on resilience and how to build it – is also brilliantly useful for working with young people. And then there are the people in your community who, right now, might be doing great things.

One of the people I have learned most from recently is Richard Marshall, the manager of Halifax rugby league team. At the start of the season he was forced to gather all the players into a room and persuade them to take a 10 per cent pay cut as the team was in such financial difficulty. Rugby players aren't paid a lot anyway, especially given the shortness of their careers. Imagine having to go in there and get that agreement. But he managed to do it by being direct and honest.

Halifax then lost every pre-season game plus two out of their first three matches. It was a bad, bad situation. Rugby commentators wrote them off. Everybody in the press said they would be relegated. Now, as I write this, Halifax are nearing the end of the season and are miles ahead of everyone else in terms of points. They are heading into the play-offs with a solid shot at promotion to the top league. I was privileged enough to go in and talk to the players about the power of belief and mindset. How did they turn it around? None of it was rocket science. They used the literature on mindset, on narrative, on building a common purpose, and developing strong internal communication. This is the sort of stuff that school leaders can learn from. It's great to learn from colleagues; but the world is your oyster when it comes to leadership examples.

In return, at Harrop Fold we've had visits from the NHS to see how we do team meetings (I'll explain about those in the next chapter), so it works both ways. Good leaders are mavens: they will learn from everyone.

5. It's not about competing, it's about completing

One of the worst things the government has done in the past 10 years is making schools compete with each other. It's a cliché to say that collaboration is better than competition, but it's true. Or a better way to put it is that completing on your intention is more important than competing against others.

There's a useful parable that will illustrate what I mean. Two farmers are half-way through growing season when a message comes from God telling them that although their plants look good at present a weather change is on the way. Both must immediately burn their crops then re-plough their land and re-seed their soil. The farmers are annoyed. Digging out the soil and re-planting seeds will be a lot of work given their land is growing so well. One farmer heeds the advice, but the other does not. As predicted, the weather changes and the land is destroyed. The farmer who prepared by re-seeding still gets a harvest. The other farmer, who refused to follow the word of God, is left with nothing.

This is not the end of the story, however. See, the man with all the bountiful crops doesn't laugh at his neighbour. Instead he takes him some of his bounteous crops and helps the distraught farmer to plough and seed his destroyed land. The farmer with the crops knows that when the following harvest comes both will have plenty and he can share in the fruits of the other farmer's labour should the need ever arise.

Are these two farmers competing against each other? Of course not. Each one has his own field. Just like each school leader has their own school. Plus, the farmer who follows the advice doesn't worry about the fact he got the bigger crop. That's irrelevant. All he cares about is whether everyone has enough to eat. He shares his food to create a win-win situation. He completes his own mission of making sure his crops are sorted, and he works to complete the mission of everyone else having food too.

This is how we should think about schools. We all have pupils to help and we can all do more to help others. We should be completing the mission of making sure every child is being educated, not competing over who can do it the best.

6. Leadership doesn't have to be lonely

Headteachers will often say that it's lonely at the top. But it doesn't need to be. Especially when you remember that you're not standing on top of your staff, you're just standing alongside them, willing them on.

Our school governors have been particularly good at supporting me. Not only have they given me the chance to re-imagine Harrop Fold, but they've supported me when things are challenging. They ask tough questions and give me a kick when I need it. But they'll also text me on a tough day and remind me how hard the staff have worked. In fact, just last week one texted after a difficult day and said: 'Just remember the blood, sweat and tears that went into this. We couldn't have done more.' I hope every leader has governors who are helping them out in this way. They're a vital yet often unsung part of the wider school community.

I would particularly like to mention our incredible late chair of governors, Cllr Pennington. He was a huge supporter of the school and was there for us through the bad and good times. We were lucky enough to have him open our new building, where he said Harrop Fold's turnaround was the greatest of his many achievements. We have named an area of the school after him now. He'd have really got a kick out of seeing the *Educating...* series. His resilience, along with the rest of the governing body, was so important to making the school you see on television today.

The reason why headteachers sometimes feel lonely is they can tend to believe they must have all the answers to a problem. Yet heads are surrounded by so many different people with different experiences that it's almost never the case you will be the best person to solve a problem. When I asked everyone in the staff to come up with money-saving ideas, it wasn't just because I wanted to get their buy-in for the solutions but because I knew they would have much better ideas than me. Luckily, I don't find that hard to admit. I know some heads like to keep a level of mystique, but I like to listen to others. That's what stops the job from being lonely.

7. Stand up for the profession

One of the people I most admire in education at the moment is Dame Alison Peacock who is heading up the new Chartered College of Teaching. The organisation has taken some flak from people confused about why it is needed, but I think it is vital that the teaching profession starts standing up for itself.

In particular, I believe everyone in the schools community needs to recognise how changes over the past decade are setting up many of the most vulnerable kids to fail. The new, harder, GCSEs have been really tough for a lot of our kids who, like me, find exams a real challenge. We know from the data that white working-class kids are among the worst performers in the country, particularly the boys. This is the demographic that we teach and we want to improve results. But, so far, no one has any solution for what to do about this.

Instead, school leaders in the north keep hearing about the brilliant transformation of London schools. It is true that results were dire a decade ago in the capital, and now they are great. A range of factors play into that, though. A simple example is that changes to the way schools are now measured means there is an emphasis on children learning a foreign language. In London, many pupils start school already speaking two languages – that's a huge advantage for language GCSEs. Children in London are also more likely to have immigrant parents who tend to be aspirational for their children's education and to spend more money on private additional tuition. School leaders in white working-class communities are more likely to teach pupils with limited skills and to have parents who protectively tell their children that school doesn't matter (to the extent we have even had parents take their children on holiday instead of them turning up to a maths GCSE).

There are deep cultural differences in the way that school and education is prioritised across the country which cannot be wished away by fiddling about with the league tables. Even worse, I think we are going to see the country going backwards in terms of the progress that has been made for closing the achievement gap between poorer children and their peers in wealthier families.

The new GCSE reforms – in which there is now a new super-duper top grade 9 – privileges the few children smart enough to get the very top grade. This year around 2,000 children got the very top score in all their core subjects. How many were in comprehensives? The more differentiation at the top, the more it is likely to benefit the children whose parents can afford private tutors and, as research from the Sutton Trust commonly shows, those children are disproportionately in private schools.

What of the pupils like me? If I was faced with these GCSEs, and only able to do a very academic curriculum because of government pressures, I would not have gone to university. I wouldn't have been able to work those two hours a day to get my degree. I wouldn't have become a headteacher and I wouldn't have helped turned around this community. That's the truth of it. Hence, my worry is that in 10 years' time we will be back in a situation where children from low-income families are more disenfranchised from higher education than ever before and the private school kids will be once again dominating the professions.

Before anyone accuses me of having low expectations here, let me be clear: I think our kids are capable of doing amazing things. I'm not writing any child off as 'non-academic' or anything like that. I have a problem with the way that services are being stripped out and our job made more difficult while cities like London get praise and additional cash, even though they need it less.

As a school, we serve a complex community, some of whom rely on mental health services, council housing, probation officers, and anti-social behaviour enforcement teams, to keep their world together. That's the reality of a community where jobs are scarce or uncertain – especially in this day of zero-hour contracts. We work with all our pupils on improving their grit, resilience, and mental toughness. But they are facing a lot of challenges in their lives and it is getting worse. Social services are disappearing. We have had no regeneration in the local area. We do a lot to hold back the tide in the face of this but longer term I really do believe there will be trouble if young people feel increasingly disenfranchised in a qualifications system that only values a certain type of academic learning.

Ultimately, the way I see it, in the school system right now, clever boy Ross would be okay and naughty boy Drew would not succeed. So I salute people like Dame Alison Peacock who are setting up organisations to help teachers stand up against policies implemented in a punitive way against our kids. And I applaud people like Jill Wood, the headteacher in the North-East who refused to give her pupils the SAT exams in their last year at primary school as she felt they were unnecessary and diminishing their learning. As the Malcolm X saying goes, 'A man who stands for nothing will fall for everything,' and our kids deserve better than that.

8. Nothing comes without risk

When the *Educating Greater Manchester* opportunity came along I spent a long time thinking about the potential downfalls. People often wonder what makes a school leader agree to having hundreds of cameras put up around their school given the potential for things to go wrong is huge. What if you lose your temper at a pupil? What if a teacher doesn't behave in the way you want them to behave?

In the end, no action comes without risk. If Harrop Fold had turned down the opportunity to be in the television show then, yes, we'd have avoided any potential negative publicity, but we would also have limited our potential for telling our story. We would never be able to talk about our debt. We wouldn't have a permanent record of how amazing our staff and pupils really are. In my case the series is enabling me to do more paid speaking gigs at businesses, awards ceremonies, and leadership conferences. Speaking gigs which will help pay back that debt!

So there's a risk in doing the television show and there's a risk in not doing it. The problem is that our brain's negativity bias pings more strongly when something bad happens. Hence, we avoid trying to do anything that's bad. One way to do that is to do little. That way no one can blame us when things go wrong. But inaction is still action. Not doing the television show could have left the story of Harrop Fold untold, and that seemed a waste. Hence, we grasped the nettles and got on with it. Sometimes that's the best thing you can do.

9. Ofsted is just one piece of information

People get really hung up on the judgements of Ofsted, the school inspectorate, but in the end it is just one piece of information. Inspectors aren't there, day-in and day-out, while teachers and school leaders are working with the community to change education. Inspectors don't see the relationships developed with pupils over a whole year. At best, they see a couple of days and talk to a handful of pupils.

One of the things that's great about the *Educating...* series is that it shows how a school works over a whole year. That's really important. The way a pupil is in September is very different to how they behave by Easter or by the end of the year. Likewise, as a teacher, you go on your own journey each year. Some things go well, some things go badly. Any inspector turning up halfway through the process can't see how things will turn out in the end. A good leader has to keep faith in their vision for the future and be realistic, but optimistic, about how things will turn out.

Back in 2013 when the Ofsted inspectors turned up I was focused on ensuring they could see what we are trying to do in our school. If you look at our results, they don't always look fantastic. Compared to some other schools they look low. In part, that's because we don't exclude any young people. It's also because the pupils turn up with lower average grades when they start at the school and because we are fighting battles other schools don't have to face (like paying back our huge over-hanging debt). Factors like that are important: every bit as much as exam results and exercise books.

We are aware that Ofsted are due any time back to Harrop and that we could face our grade reducing. In some ways, this doesn't bother me because I don't think the Ofsted grade is why people choose our school. Parents send their children to us because they know we will keep them safe and help them to progress socially and academically. We therefore have to console ourselves with knowing that Ofsted is just one piece of information. Many other pieces of information matter just as much, if not more: the views of parents, the thoughts of our governors, our attendance rate, our exclusions record, how many times a year a kid is able to grasp a new idea, or the kids we see going on to achieve well and coming back to teach with us.

Ofsted matters, but it's not the most important thing. Not even close to it.

10. Giving hope during difficult times is a valuable skill

Academically, I am average on a good day. As a manager, I've learned lots about efficient and smart operations. But as a leader I'm really good at one thing: giving hope during difficult times. And that's a skill people don't always value, but they should.

The bombing of the Ariana Grande concert in Manchester shook our community to the core. How can anyone be so spiteful as to kill innocent bystanders? Especially children? A number of our pupils were at the event and really shaken by it. As the *Educating...* series showed, we moved to get counselling support and help those pupils as best as possible.

After that terrible event, I was also impressed by Chief Constable Ian Hopkins who behaved in the most courageous and inspirational way. Each day he would be on the radio or television reassuring the people of Manchester about their safety and the ongoing investigations. Hopkins spread the messages we all needed to hear. 'Hope not fear' reminded the people of Manchester of our responsibility not to start pointing fingers at our neighbours, but to look out for one another in such desperate times. The concerts organised in the city, just a week later, were testament to the fact we are all stronger when we work together.

When I got to Harrop Fold, the most important thing the headteacher Anthony and I did was instil in people a belief that the school could turn around. We made people believe it was possible to re-imagine the school in a better way. We did this through an almost mind-numbingly simple combination of turning up every day, listening to people, and enthusiastically modelling how we wanted the staff and pupils to behave. Sounds easy when put like that, doesn't it? Having the energy to do it can be much more difficult.

That's why having a purpose is so important. On the dark, damp, wintry mornings, when you know a long day awaits, it is much easier to get up and get on when you remember that Harrop Fold is 'making *the* difference'. Cold mornings aren't pleasurable; but making a difference is.

My advice to any headteacher taking up the reins at a new school is to think about how they will spread hope. What's the key message you will repeat to staff? How will you make them believe that even though a day looks challenging, by the end of it that teacher, or caretaker, or receptionist, is going to be able to go away knowing they contributed to an important mission?

Spreading hope is a vital skill. Ignore it at your peril.

Chapter 11 –
The Harrop Fold Playbook:
How we make the difference

In sport, the phrase 'playbook' refers to a manual describing the tactics a team will use to beat their opposition. American football teams, in particular, use playbooks to make sure each member of the team knows exactly what to do when the ball goes into play.

For any business, it's a good idea to know your 'playbook'. Below is ours. Every school, company, or sports team needs to adapt to their own circumstance. But I hope by sharing our playbook it might give you some ideas for re-imagining your own school, business or community.

The Harrop Fold Playbook

Our values

There are three values underlying what we are doing at Harrop Fold:

- Putting people first
- Living the purpose
- Re-imagine not rebuild

If these sound a bit complex, there's an easier way to think about them:

People > purpose > process

The 3Ps are a classic piece of management theory and definitely not devised by me! Every organisation needs the right people, following the same purpose, completing a series of processes.

At Harrop, we do this by making sure we pick people with the right skills and strengths, we hold a shared purpose, and have processes for constantly re-imagining how we might do things better.

Our method for leadership by wandering about

As mentioned earlier in the book (Chapter 6) one of the most important aspects of our playbook at Harrop Fold is the concept of walking around the school. Leaders need to be seen, on the ground, gathering information and solving problems as they go.

There is no substitute for walking around school in order to find out what is going on.

Our method for communication across Team Harrop

Correctly managing communication across a team is one of the most important skills in the leadership toolkit. One thing I wish had known about before becoming a headteacher is Google's Project Aristotle.

A major problem for education is that too many schools focus on trying to recruit a 'hero head'. Great leaders are important but schools are not run by one person. They operate via teams. Hence, the whole school is a team. Then, within that, there are smaller teams. Each department is a team. Each classroom is a team.

Google, one of the most successful organisations on the entire planet, realised back in 2012 that leaders were what was making the biggest differences in their businesses. Teams were driving innovation. So, Google asked, what makes a great team?

First, they assumed it would be the people. Certain configurations of personalities would surely yield successful teams? Yet no pattern emerged.

In the end, Google worked out the best teams are those who operate within an agreed set of behaviours. Who is on the team matters much less than how the team works together. This was something I instinctively knew from sport and from teaching. It's not about who is in the classroom, it's about how people interact. But it was great to have that tacit knowledge confirmed by such thorough research!

Over time, we have changed the way everyone in the school talks to one another. Not just in terms of psychological safety, which I've talked about before, but also in terms of structure. We now have a meetings playbook.

The four types of meeting

In the book *Death by Meetings*, Patrick Lencioni shows that so many meetings in businesses are totally useless. It's true! One of the major problems of meetings is that everyone turns up with a different view of what they are for. Some people think meetings are for giving information. Others think they are discussions. Yet others think it is time for creative exploration, or some pull it to operational task-based chat. There are too many different things happening for the time to be productive.

Hence, at Harrop Fold we now have four types of meetings and we are very clear about their purpose and what activities we will do during them.

It works on Lencioni's finding that there are four types of effective meetings:

- Daily five-minute briefings
- Weekly one-hour operational talks
- Monthly several-hour strategic meeting
- Quarterly whole-day evaluation meeting

We encourage every faculty to run meetings of these four types and we run them at senior level too.

The senior leaders' meeting structure

Daily briefings

Every day, the senior leadership team have a five-minute, standing, information-only meeting. I like to think of it as a series of 30-second news clips. High-level, very quick. They are chaired by different people and we sometimes have an amusing starter just to get everyone awake and listening.

Weekly operational

These are one-hour meetings where we talk through issues that need action.

At the start, everyone gives a round-up of their biggest issues. We jot these down, then prioritise, and hash out solutions and actions over the hour.

Monthly strategic meeting

We have these around every three to four weeks, depending on the length of the term. They are multi-hour and we focus on one issue and come prepared to talk about it and make decisions.

For example, we might think about resilience. How can we build resilience in ourselves, our pupils, and the school more broadly? In advance of the session, the leader will send around some reading. At the start of the session we might do an activity, such as a resilience test. And then for the remainder of the session we get to the bottom of the issue and make decisions.

Termly evaluation reviews

These are zoom-out sessions which take around five or six hours and involves the whole team examining how we are meeting our objectives, how our team is doing and any other issues we need to evaluate.

Whole-school strategy meeting

At the whole-school level we have headline meetings twice a week, which are five-minute, quick-fire information round-ups. On Thursdays we do messages at the start but add in good news for 10 minutes, to reinforce the good stuff and deal with the negativity bias.

I also added a weekly 'joint leaders meeting'. Over the years at Harrop I noticed that senior and middle leaders don't often get into a room all together. So, in 2014, I started a meeting every Wednesday morning, from 8am to 8.20am, in which all leaders – at every level – come together and chew over an issue. It's good for heads of departments (for example, head of geography or head of year 9) to see the senior team discussing an issue. In return, the senior leaders are able to get information from middle leaders about the reasons why a policy is, or is not, working.

Don't use written minutes; use a live board

One thing we don't use at Harrop Fold is written minutes. I think minutes are really stupid. Some people think I'm a heretic for saying this. They want to see all the conversations in a school neatly printed up on paper. But research suggests that hardly anyone reads the minutes. Instead, people spend the beginning of meetings going over the minutes, which is a waste of time. I am too impatient for that!

Instead of minutes, we therefore use something called a 'live board'. I prefer to see things drawn visually so at each meeting we nominate someone to write onto a flipchart as we are discussing items and making decisions. This surprises lots of people but, as you'll have seen in films about sport, it's a really common practice all across the world, and for good reason. The visual nature of bigger writing on a flipchart is easier to remember. It's also a more immediate outcome to the discussions taking place in a meeting too. Seeing ideas taking shape in front of people in the meeting is very motivating and helps with encouraging good decision-making. In this age of mobile phones, it's also easy to take a photograph of the live board once the meeting ends. That way you can send it to everyone immediately. No waiting for someone to type up what was said. No waiting for the printer so you can take bundles of minutes to the next meeting. Just write up what is discussed and agreed on a flipchart. Take a photo. Email the photo. Job done.

Find your own path

As I mentioned earlier in the book, one of the biggest problems my brother Ross faced when he first started teaching at Harrop was that he tried to be someone he's not. Leaders need to be authentic. I cannot stress that enough. Each person is valuable in their own way. There's no point pretending to be something that you're not because the kids always sniff out a fake.

My style of leadership works in the context of Harrop Fold. I wouldn't want to be a headteacher anywhere else. If I'm honest, I'm not sure I'd even be a great headteacher in some other places. Without the same sense of moral purpose, I don't think I could do the job.

Having the confidence to back who you truly are is therefore the final part of The Harrop Fold Playbook. Be your honest best self. That's who the kids will respond to. That's who staff will respond to. It's scary, and it makes you vulnerable, but until you are willing to tell the difficult stories about yourself – reveal your own wobbly rabbits and daft moments of wedging your brother into a van – then people won't respond to you. We are all humans walking down this crazy path called life. You've got to find your own way down it. There is no other route.

Chapter 12 – Where do we go from here?

'Your most important work is always ahead of you, never behind you' – Steven Covey

One of my favourite stories is Aesop's fable of the hare and the tortoise because I can relate to the tortoise. But there's another useful Aesop story called 'The Boy and the Filberts'. (Filberts is an ancient name for hazelnuts). In the story, a boy puts his hand into a jar full of the delicious nuts. Grabbing as many as he can, the boy fills his fist to the brim. But when he tries to remove his hand, it gets stuck. The neck of the pitcher is too narrow to allow a fist out. The boy bursts into tears. Unwilling to let go of a single nut, he can never remove his hand.

The moral of the story is that unless you can become satisfied with less then you may not be able to move on. It's a heartbreaking allegory for a leader, like myself and my staff, who want to do more for the kids that we work with.

Sometimes, however, you cannot do it all. At Harrop Fold, we've done great things, but the debt has undoubtedly affected what we can offer the pupils, and that's why I've become so angry about it.

We have held back the tide and kept as many of the hazelnuts in our hands as we can, but there's no doubt that our results are now being affected by the crazy situation we find ourselves in. We cannot keep having huge class sizes and fewer members of staff without some kickback.

That's not an excuse for our results, by the way. In the past few years we found the shift in the way schools are measured to be tricky. Many of our students thrived on vocational courses, but those courses are no longer allowed to count in the performance tables. The changes made by government so that all exams are taken at the end of the course was also a tough transition.

If we could join an academy trust then we could get help with these things but, for now, the £1.7 million debt hangs around our neck and stops that progress.

So, what's next for me and Harrop Fold? I want to get that debt paid off. It's that simple. I want to find a way to wipe the debt off our books. Maybe a business person or a philanthropist will write us a cheque – that would be ideal.

Until then, I'm doing as many talks as I can to businesses, or leaders, or anyone, who can help with this situation. With an increased profile from *Educating Greater Manchester* I am hoping I can get more speaking gigs to help raise the cash. That's one reason I have become executive headteacher from this year, and will be handing the operational reins over to my team (including Ross).

I also want to encourage people to start thinking more strategically about education. Too many people don't think 5 or 10 years into the future. The cuts to public services in our local area are decimating the progress we are making in our schools. Complex communities require complex resources. Sometimes a liaison officer needs to go and work with a family. Maybe counselling is needed. Or mediation. All of this can have a dramatic positive effect on the results of children.

And yet. Budget cuts in local authorities continue year-on-year. We are amazing at what we do, but we aren't miracle-workers. It sometimes feels like our arm is being yanked out of the nut jar and we are going to have no choice but to drop a few.

For me, that's unthinkable. I am not going to let kids sit at home because other schools have excluded them. I am not going to give up on engaging with social workers, police officers, and all the other public services who help our children. These days we go and do the home visits to sort issues out, because if not us, then who?

Which is what worries me about the school's future. If we cannot wipe the debt, and the results dip, then we face either being forced to close or to join an academy trust that might not have the same ethos as we have developed. Closing the school would be dire. It is at the heart of the community. What would it say to close a brand-new building that's less than a decade old?

If the school goes to an academy trust, the local community will not get to choose which one takes over. Some are excellent. Consilium Trust, who we actively want to join, are great. But if the school is pushed forcibly into a takeover then any trust could be put in charge and a new headteacher will likely be installed. Will that headteacher sit on the community committees? Will they be able to calm down warring parents? Will they keep the hard lads on the straight and narrow? Results matter, but other things are just as important in Little Hulton and we must not forget them.

All this said, Team Harrop are taking lots of action to improve results. I don't believe in sitting around pontificating. I believe in doing. As my parents always said, 'Don't just stand there, do something.'

In my impatience over the past couple of years, I set out a big list of changes I want. Some of that hasn't worked. I was too quick to act and didn't spend time really looking at the problems and really understanding the possible solutions. This, I know now, was a big mistake and one I will avoid making again in the future.

One thing I don't want us to ease back on is having the school open for pupils beyond normal schooling hours. Not least because it enables us to provide a better diet than some pupils get at home. But we are going to have to pull back on some other things. For example, our staff now work at weekends, and in holidays, and they do an extra period each day. That's too much, of course; we won't ban people from working extra hours but we will be sitting down and making some decisions about how we manage this workload more sustainably rather than engaging in a group think where we all egg each other on to do more simply for the sake of it rather than because it aids performance. Leadership means taking a step back sometimes: zooming out and deciding if it's sensible to carry on. I always want us to keep being honest when things are not working, and keep tweaking until we get the needed marginal gains.

Finally, I want to get better at working out how to listen even better. The best teachers spend time at the beginning of a lesson working out where their pupils are in their learning journey. Those teachers figure out whether children know information or not, and if they are ready to take in more. In sports, and schools, leaders tend to miss this step. We can bolsh in with our ready-made plans and fail to consider if staff are ready to take on board our messages, or if the staff are tuned out because they have heard our message a million times before. If you're telling staff to check pupil uniform, and it is not being done regularly and consistently, the good leader will find out why the message isn't being taken on board, rather than hand out another edict. (Is it because the teachers think uniform is unimportant? Or that it won't be followed up?)

You've got to assume nothing and ask everything if you want to be a good leader.

'Change will not come if we wait for some other person. We are the one's we've been waiting for. We are the changes we seek' – Barack Obama

Working at Harrop Fold is the most exhausting, exhilarating, exciting thing in the world. The team make it come alive. The kids make it worthwhile. It is a privilege to be there every day.

This week, on Saturday, I will buy a lottery ticket and pray that it's a winner so the school's debt can be paid off. On Monday, when inevitably the ticket is thrown in the bin, I will be grateful for the chance to go to Harrop and make the difference anyway.

As I drive along the motorway, on my way in, I'll probably think about how unlikely it is that the naughty boy who was once almost excluded from primary school finally came good in the end. And then I'll think, as I so often do, about Mrs Firth and how she changed my life. How Mr Morgan, and Mrs Fry, and Mr Harris, and Fred Shadwell, and Anthony Edkins, all helped change the course of my life.

The *Educating…* series carries on this tradition by showing how teachers change the lives of children. And I am so very proud that in this year's show the world will see how three brothers – plus a cast of thousands – are helping carry on that tradition.

I told you something special was happening in Little Hulton. We are making *the* difference.

Acknowledgements

Thanks to:

Laura for your invaluable support, insight and for help in 'shaping the voice'!

Helen Woodward for original drafts, interviews and believing in the school.

Tracey Llewellyn for inspiring ideas and for championing Team Harrop.

The truly brilliant and inspirational Harrop Fold Governing Body for unswerving support and tenacity in pushing Team Harrop to *make the difference.*

Mum, Dad, Ross, Ben and the extended family.

Vicki, Tom, Fin and Max for your love, support and belief. Nothing could have been achieved without you!